THE ITALIAN LAKES

Aubrey Feist

THE ITALIAN LAKES

B. T. Batsford Ltd
London and Sydney

For Kay

First published 1975

Made and printed in Great Britain by
Cox & Wyman Ltd, London, Fakenham and Reading
for the publishers B. T. Batsford Ltd,
4 Fitzhardinge Street, London W1
and 23 Cross Street, Brookvale, NSW 2100, Australia

ISBN 0 7134 2975 5

Contents

The Plates

Acknowledgments

The publishers wish to thank the following for supplying photographs reproduced in this book:

Bavaria-Verlag for plates 9, 15 and 16
J. Allan Cash for plates 2 and 5
Douglas Dickins for plates 4, 6–8 and 10–13
A. F. Kersting for plate 14
Kenneth Scowen for plate 3
The Swiss National Tourist Office for plate 1

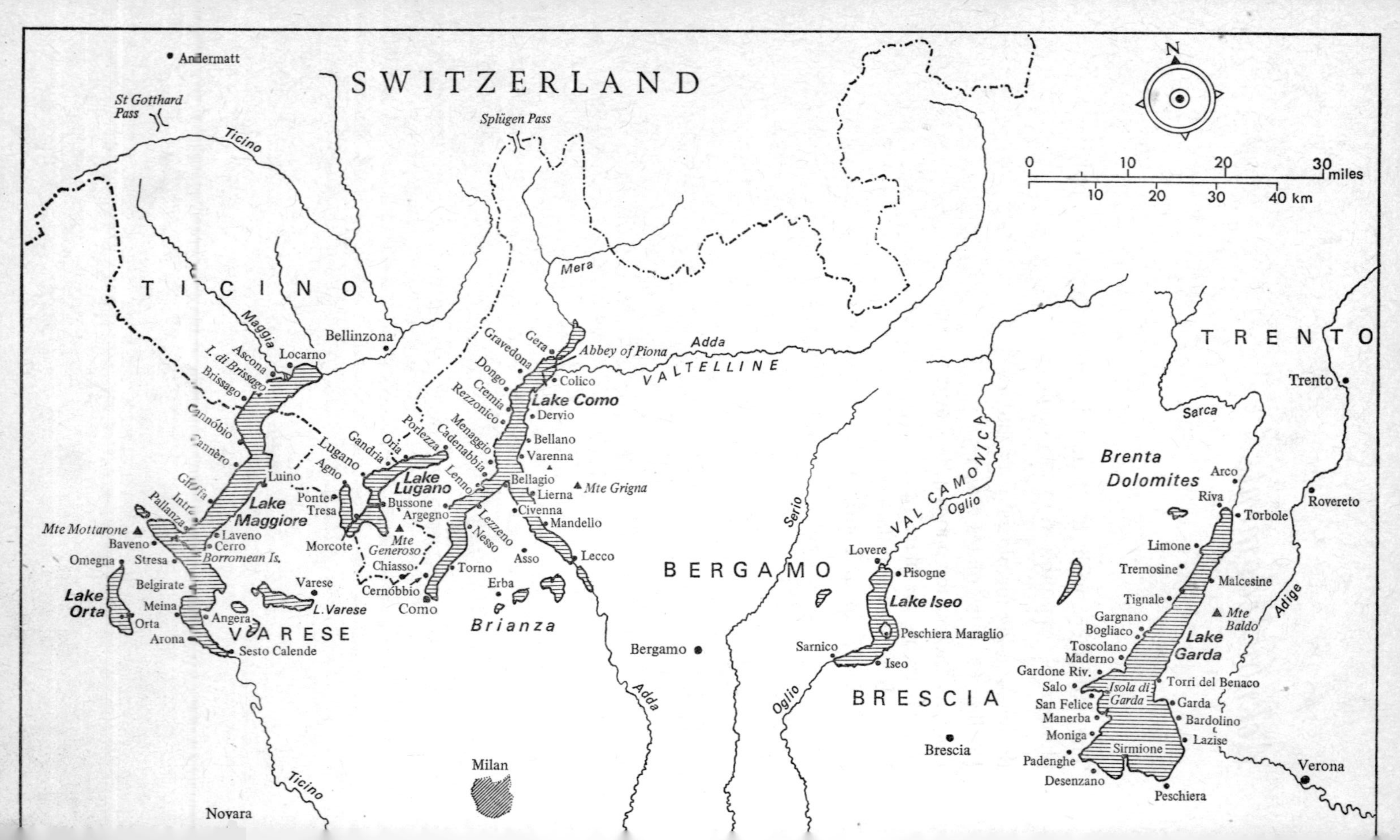
SWITZERLAND
Andermatt
St Gotthard Pass
Splügen Pass
N
0
10
20
30 miles
10
20
30
40 km
Ticino
Mera
TICINO
Maggia
Bellinzona
Locarno
Ascona
I. di Brissago
Brissago
Cannóbio
Cannèro
Ghiffa
Intra
Pallanza
Luino
Lake Maggiore
Mte Mottarone
Baveno
Laveno
Cerro
Omegna
Stresa
Borromean Is.
Belgirate
Lake Orta
Meina
Orta
Angera
Arona
VARESE
Sesto Calende
Varese
L. Varese
Lugano
Agno
Ponte Tresa
Gandria
Oria
Porlezza
Lake Lugano
Bussone
Argegno
Morcote
Mte Generoso
Chiasso
Cernóbbio
Como
Gera
Gravedona
Dongo
Cremia
Rezzonico
Menaggio
Cadenabbia
Lenno
Abbey of Piona
Adda
Colico
VALTELLINE
Lake Como
Dervio
Bellano
Varenna
Bellagio
Mte Grigna
Lierna
Civenna
Mandello
Lezzeno
Nesso
Torno
Asso
Erba
Lecco
Brianza
Milan
Novara
Ticino
Adda
BERGAMO
Bergamo
Serio
VAL CAMONICA
Oglio
Lovere
Pisogne
Lake Iseo
Peschiera Maraglio
Sarnico
Iseo
Oglio
BRESCIA
Brescia
TRENTO
Trento
Sarca
Rovereto
Brenta Dolomites
Arco
Riva
Torbole
Limone
Tremosine
Malcesine
Adige
Tignale
Mte Baldo
Gargnano
Bogliaco
Lake Garda
Toscolano
Maderno
Gardone Riv.
Salo
Isola di Garda
Torri del Benaco
San Felice
Garda
Manerba
Bardolino
Moniga
Lazise
Sirmione
Padenghe
Desenzano
Peschiera
Verona

Foreword

'Lake Maggiore is a gem, the most brilliant gem, perhaps, of all those adorning Italy's northern crown.' That is what a romantic said of one of the great lakes which lie between the Alps and the Po Valley, and the description could with equal justice be applied to the others.

If there is one thing more than another that I remember about this delightful land, it is the marvellously clear air which, in spring and summer, sharpens every outline and turns the water deep green or blue, in which clouds and mountains are mirrored. The intensity of colour is increased in the hot sunshine. Baskets of fruit under the arcades become vivid splashes of orange and yellow. Lakeside villages become 'double' villages – twin patterns of grey, cream and russet: the one clinging to the rocky ledge on which it has drowsed for centuries, the other reflected just as clearly in the water which laps its foundations.

Opinions differ as to the best month in which to visit the Italian Lakes, but for garden lovers I would suggest May. I was there last in the middle of June, when the azaleas, oleanders, rhododendrons and magnolias were over. But it is well worth going there at any time of the year.

On the Lakes those picturesque fishing-boats called *luciè* still carry their awnings stretched over half-hoops of iron, while efficient little streamers and hydrofoils ply from point to point. There are mountain strongholds and villages which look as if they had grown out of the rock. There are ancient cities to explore: Milan, Brescia, Bergamo, Verona – even Venice is within comparatively easy reach. And here in the country of the Lakes, History has not been idle. Condottieri have led their armies of mercenaries through the vineyards and olive orchards to fight for the Winged Lion of Venice or the Viper of Milan; in nearly every place you visit you will find a memorial to Garibaldi and his Redshirts, while at the little town of Dongo on the northern arm of Lake Como, Mussolini was taken by the partisans when only a few miles from the safety of the Swiss frontier, leaving the legend of his treasure to swell the store of local folklore.

There is something for everyone. For the sophisticated, luxurious hotels – though most of those bordering the Lakes are shut during the winter-sports season in the mountains, splendid motor-roads, bars, bathing *lidi* where beautiful bodies are basted and grilled, music, sailing, and water-skiing, while for those who enjoy gambling there is a good casino in the Italian enclave of Campione on Lake Lugano. Those who are interested will find palaces and castles, each with its own story; and always – or nearly always – the pellucid air and sunshine of Italy.

Finally, I would like to make it clear that this book does not aspire to be either a guide-book or a history. It is simply a record of journeys spaced over a good many years, together with such observations and scraps of local lore as I have noted on the spot or found stored in my memory.

1. Lake Maggiore

The Northern Arm

Of all the visits that I have made to the Lakes of Northern Italy, the most enjoyable have been in the company of my wife Kay. Together, we once walked over the Alps and came down to rest at Lugano; together, and at our leisure without a thought of writing a book about them, we have spent lazy, delightful holidays on the shores of Lugano, Garda and Como; and together, only a short time ago, we stayed at Pallanza which – with the neighbouring town of Stresa – is the most central and convenient base from which to explore Maggiore.

With regard to the relative merits of the greater lakes, one cannot afford to be dogmatic. Each to his choice, and the choice is an extremely personal matter. It all depends on your idea of a holiday, on what you want to see and do. If you have a passion for sun-bathing or such sports as sailing and water-skiing, then I am not your man. But if, like me, you are fond of walking or, alternatively, a confirmed potterer with a love of the old and picturesque and an enthusiasm for ferreting out queer little facts of history – well, then we are of a like mind and I may be able to help you.

As for priorities, many people would award the prize for beauty to Como, and that for historical interest to the somewhat isolated Lake Garda; but in the Land of the Three Lakes – I Tre Laghi – meaning Lugano, Como and Maggiore, many of us would agree that for a combination of the two qualities, it is difficult to beat the last named, where you can gaze at the breath-taking beauty of the Borromean Islands or the view across the Lombard Plain from Monte Mottarone, while for the story of the colourful past you have the Borromeï, the somewhat chequered history of the Visconti of Milan, and memories of the Garibaldini with their long hair, their high-crowned Calabrian hats and waving plumes, who fought so valiantly for freedom just over a 100 years ago.

So, as any more definite attempt to allocate the palm would be futile, we will content ourselves with visiting each of the great lakes in turn, beginning with Maggiore and staying, I would suggest, at one of those excellent hotels on the Gulf of Pallanza. The last time that my wife and I went to Italy was under the wing of the Compagna Italia Turismo (C.I.T.), so we enjoyed all the advantages of a sensible package which looked after the boring business of air travel and accommodation but did not deprive us of our independence. Pallanza is one of the C.I.T. centres, and from there we were able to branch out in all directions. But first a few facts and figures.

Five-sixths of the Lake is in Italy and one-sixth is in the Swiss canton of Ticino. The west bank is Piedmontese and the east is in the Lombard province of Varese. Travellers from England usually go by air to Milan or Turin, or by the international road and rail route through the Simplon Pass. I must warn you, however, that at the time of writing there is no ordinary bus service round the shores of the Lake and that unless you have a car, you are entirely dependent on the steamers and your own legs. The steamers are very convenient; and, for a reasonable sum, you can buy a three-day or weekly season ticket, which is a first-rate investment.

As is usual in these lakes, the water is deep. The authorities differ, but a fair estimate of the maximum depth of Maggiore would be 1,250 feet (380 m). The length is about 40 miles (64 km) and the width varies from 5 to 6 miles (8-9½ km). The Lake is fed by a number of small streams, while the Ticino River traverses it from north to south. It enters the Lake cold and green from the Alps, but it is bright blue and navigable when it emerges at Sesto Calende to join the Po below Pavia.

Maggiore is noted for its magnificent and variegated scenery. It is bounded by granite mountains except to the south, where there are low hills and vineyards. Half-way along there is that great central bulge known as the Gulf of Pallanza – one of the loveliest parts of the Lake, where the towering massif of the Alps rises far away above the water and, in the foreground, the Borromean Islands glow like bright galleons riding at anchor.

You must not imagine that it is always the serene blue of the travel advertisements. Maggiore has its winds: the Tramontaro which comes roaring down from Switzerland, the Inverno which blows from the south, and the western Mergozzo. They can lash the Lake into a grey fury but usually its waters are green and placid. The coloured villas and villages on the shore quiver in the heat-haze, and one can forget the wind-breaks which protect the orchards and vineyards, and those rare angry moods when the sky darkens and the lashing rain drives before the gale. But even this is worth seeing.

The Gulf of Pallanza is bounded on the north by a small peninsula, one either side of which are the resorts of Suna and Intra, connected by a road running along the shore, and dominated by the delightful old town of Pallanza which lies on the tip of the headland between them. Together with the village of Fondotoce, they form the commune of Pallanza-Verbania. The climate is mild and sunny and the whole peninsula is rich in semi-tropical trees and shrubs which riot in the villa gardens and along the spacious promenades down by the shore, where the oleander holds pride of place.

The waterfront of Pallanza is like most modern water-fronts – shops and hotels, but leading from it are steep, narrow alleys of ochre-coloured houses – many with iron balconies, gay with flowers, and some of them built on rough outcrops of rock. The old arcaded buildings of the Piazza Pedroni are interesting, but the heart of Pallanza is the Piazza Garibaldi, and this too is down by the Lake. Here you will find the Town Hall, the

Market, and the modernized fifteenth-century church of San Leonardo with its great grey campanile dating from 1689 and dominating the whole town. Like so many Italian churches, the interior is dark and gloomy – at least, to our eyes; but there is a magnificent pulpit of black wood, richly carved, and a dim altar which is most impressive. From here the Via Cavour leads up the hill to the Piazza Antonio Grimschi – a central point from which radiate broad avenues: one to Intra, one to Suna, and one – the Viale Antonio Azari, which is a continuation of the Via Cavour and leads to the church of Madonna di Campagna, with its Romanesque bell-tower and its frescoes. This lies at the foot of Monte Rosa, so, if you are energetic enough, you can climb to the summit and have a rest in the little oratory of Santa Croce. If you are aged, infirm, or merely lazy, you can reach the foot of the mountain in a few minutes by car.

In ancient times, on the high ground of Castagnola which forms the tip of the peninsula, the Celts founded a settlement – and that was the beginning of this fine modern town with its villas, shops and hotels. The Roman legionaries followed, but encamped on more level ground near the shore, and it was here that, later, the medieval Pallanza began. In the Museum you can see a *cippus* or carved pillar dedicated to Roman goddesses. This was excavated in the seventeenth century near the High Altar of San Stephano, and proves that this church, like the little twelfth-century church of San Remigio, was built on the site of a heathen temple.

You should go to San Remigio to see this church, restored in the sixteenth century by Girolamo Appiano, whose ruffed and bearded effigy adorns the nave; but, unfortunately, the Villa Remigio is now in private ownership. The little church is a national monument but we did not find it easily. Misdirected more than once, we made two attempts, but the second only succeeded after we had toiled up hills and narrow cobbled lanes between garden walls for over an hour in the hot sunshine. Kay has a good sense of direction but she was not at the top of her form that morning, and we must have walked in a circle half-way to Intra and back. And all the time, if we had only known it, there was a very small notice-board in the Piazza San Guiseppe which would have told us how to get there by a short cut. The church looks grey and rather desolate, for it is very small and hoary with age. It is open from 3 until 7 o'clock; but if, as we did, you find it shut, you can see nearly all there is to see through a large iron grille. We found that tiring walk worth while.

I have heard that the grounds of the Villa Remigio remind one of an English park, for the lay-out is restrained and lacks that flamboyance which to a northerner can be unpleasing. As I have said, the gardens are no longer open to the public, but not far away is the Villa Taranto which attracts scientists and gardeners from all over the world. It is easy to reach from Pallanza and even has its own pier so, if you wish to do so, you can travel the short distance by steamer, while for those who come from farther afield there are bus services from Milan and Turin, and a daily bus service from Lugano and from Locarno at the northern end of the Lake.

Its history is romantic. The late Captain Neil McEacharn, a Scottish gentleman and a member of the Queen's Bodyguard in Scotland – the Royal Company of Archers – was a descendant of Marshal MacDonald, son of an exiled Jacobite family, whom Napoleon created Duke of Taranto. So when Captain McEacharn built his house and laid out his wonderful botanical garden in what had been wasteland, he named it in honour of his illustrious ancestor – the Villa Taranto. When he died, in 1964, wishing to perpetuate his work, he generously bequeathed the property to the Italian Government, but it has been open to the public since 1952.

The Captain was buried in a mausoleum in the great garden that he loved, not far from the little Roman Catholic chapel in which Mass is celebrated each Sunday. There is a laboratory and a school of gardening, and congresses and meetings are held at the Villa. The gardens themselves are wonderfully landscaped, with terraces, lotus and lily ponds, waterfalls, and over 20,000 specimens of rare and exotic plants brought from all parts of the world and acclimatized with loving skill and care. And yet these gardens, too, have been likened to the great parks of England.

A few years ago I would have said that another 'must' at Pallanza was the fine collection of peasant costumes in the Palazzo Dugnani. But, to our disgust, we found that, like the Villa Remigio, they are no longer on view. We were disappointed at not being able to see them, for they must have been very interesting and beautiful, though perhaps a little sad. The traditional costumes are still not entirely unknown: we have seen them several times on elderly women from mountain villages. But these are the days of unisex shirt and jeans, and I nearly became involved in a brawl for inadvertently addressing one long-haired young gentleman as 'Signorina'. Such a mistake could not have been made years ago, and such a collection of costumes would have helped us to realize how colourful these lakeside towns must have been in – say – the 1830s. But you cannot put the clock back and there is much to be said for the times we live in. At least you can hope to travel in Italy without being waylaid by banditti.

And yet can you? I am sorry to say that even this statement must be modified. One no longer expects to be held up within a mile of the gates of Milan; but picturesque brigandage has its modern equivalent and I think that it is worth mentioning, if only to put you on your guard. During our last visit to the Lakes, some people at our hotel left their car outside one night – the night before they started for home. In the morning they found that the rear window had been smashed and all the luggage on the back seat stolen. Even the elements had conspired to help these present-day 'banditti', for it had been a night of storm, when all other noises were drowned by the thunder. It meant delay, a badly damaged car, involvement with the police, and any amount of inconveniece. So it is wiser to leave your car empty and, above all – to insure your luggage.

1 The church of the Madonna del Sasso, Locarno

We shall return to our base at Pallanza more than once in the course of our wanderings. We shall go south from there after we have travelled north along the narrow, mountainous arm of the Lake which leads to Switzerland. But first we will cross the headland called the Punta della Castagnola and take the car-ferry from Intra across to Laveno on the eastern shore – another place well worth visiting, though it cannot compete with the beauty of Pallanza.

Set in delightful surroundings, Laveno, is primarily a communications centre and an industrial town. They make nylon and artificial silk there, and it possesses the largest pottery and porcelain factory in Italy. But the big ceramic factory on the hillside was once an Austrian barracks; the Villa Pullè, west of the town, was built on the site of an Austrian fortress, and the harbour used to be a fortified base for the Austrian gunboats which patrolled the Lake. But then came the Risorgimento – that great resurgence of the Italian people; and in 1859 there was an abortive attack on the town by Garibaldi's Piedmontese volunteers from Pallanza and Intra. The venture failed, for the Austrians had been forewarned, and a monument in the Piazza commemorates the *cacciatori* who died. It takes the form of an eagle and is a pathetic memorial, for so many of those who fell seem to have been members of the same families.

Just south of Laveno is the fishing-village of Cerro. It is still unspoiled and long may it remain so. It is only a tiny place, with no accommodation for visitors, but it will well repay a visit – as would the isolated shrine of Santa Caterina del Sasso, still farther south and only accessible by water. The shrine is a place of rare beauty: the setting for a strange story and an extraordinary natural phenomenon. Unfortunately, when we went there it was closed for repairs.

The history of St Catherine of the Rock begins as long ago as the twelfth century. In those days a certain Alberto Besozzo was one of the local bad characters, a rogue and a smuggler, with usury as a sideline. And then – quite suddenly, as is the way in legends, even well-substantiated legends like this one – came

2 *The gardens of the Isola Bella, Lake Maggiore*

retribution and remorse. One day, when Alberto was out in his boat, no doubt on some unlawful errand, the wind arose and, in the gale that followed, his little craft was overturned. In his terror he prayed for help and swore that, if he was saved, he would dedicate the rest of his life to the service of God. His prayer was answered. He was dashed ashore at the foot of an almost perpendicular cliff and somehow managed to scale the precipice as far as the little ledge or platform on which there is now a huddle of tight-packed buildings. In those days there must have been some sort of water supply – a torrent or a spring for, in fulfilment of his vow, Alberto Besozzo lived there alone, praying for forgiveness for his own and other people's sins, subsisting on roots, fruit, berries, and bread brought by his friends and lowered in a basket on the end of a rope.

And this went on for 37 years! But we must remember that this was in the Middle Ages when squalor and extreme discomfort were infallible proof of sanctity. It may seem absurd to us, even disgusting; but surely, our ancestors would have said, anyone who could sacrifice so much must be a man of God. Accordingly, when the plague came again – as it did all too often – the priests implored the Hermit of the Rock for his intercession. So the smuggler turned saint prayed to Christ and to St Catherine of Alexandria; and, sure enough, the epidemic came to an end. In gratitude for their deliverance, Alberto's neighbours built a chapel on the ledge where he lived and, after his death, this was replaced by a larger chapel to St Catherine. Still later, the Dominicans moved in; a conventual church and domestic buildings were built, and so a cult was born – the cult of the Blessed Alberto.

You would think that this was the end of the story; but you would be wrong, for a miracle was vouchsafed to the faithful. In the middle of the eighteenth century there was a tremendous fall of rock. A mass of boulders came crashing down and smashed through the roof of the little church, just above the Hermit's tomb. There the stones jammed and rested, their whole weight supported by a single great rock which, in its turn, rested on two or three ordinary bricks. And so they remained, the revered tomb undamaged, until May 1910. A miracle? You must be the judge. I am not qualified to say. But I am sure the most hardened sceptic would agree that it was remarkable.

If, as I have suggested, you visit Santa Caterina del Sasso, it will be long before you forget that cluster of sun-baked buildings poised on their narrow ledge among the fig-trees and vines, the cloisters, the slender campanile, and the dark stairs which lead straight up through a tunnel from the deep water. There is no beach. If you go in the springtime you will find the surrounding hills ablaze with laburnum; and in front of you, across the Lake with its enchanted islands, you will see the wooded heights rising to the serrated peak of Monte Rosa and, farther south, Monte Mottarone – the highest point in that long ridge called the Mergozzolo, which divides the basin of Maggiore from that of Lake Orta.

And now back to Intra on the western shore. Cavour called it the Manchester of Maggiore, but Cavour was being rude. Not that I have anything against Manchester and certainly Intra is an industrial town, but you will find nothing in it to remind you of the 'dark Satanic mills' which disfigured the England of his time. To begin with, the machinery gets its power from electricity, not coal, so there are no smoking chimneys and the air is as pure as it is up there on the rocky ledge of Santa Caterina. There are iron, rope and dye works but you would never know it. There are buildings – light, airy, bowered in roses, which look like anything but factories, yet you will find on inquiry that these charming 'palaces' and 'villas' are where they make hats, paper or soap. They are further examples of how, in design, the Italians seldom put a foot wrong.

Apart from its manufactures and the car-ferry of which the inhabitants are so proud, this thriving little place is noted for the richness of its soil, for it was built on the alluvian deposit of two mountain streams, the San Giovanni and the San Bernardino. For most of the year they are nothing to look at as streams: you might even, not unjustly, describe them as mere trickles. But when the rains come and the snow melts on the mountains, for a short time they attain the dignity of raging torrents.

On the lakeside, near the mouth of the Giovanni, there are two fine old houses, the Villa Barbò and the Villa Ada, while among the foothills behind the town there opens up the Val Introgno, famous country for walkers. Kay and I have not been there ourselves but we have heard that it is really good, with wonderful views of the Alps.

There are some excellent shops near the shore. The parish church of San Vittore, with its dome and campanile, is dark, but the East End is lighted by some good coloured windows, which glow all the more brightly for the surrounding gloom. You might also like to visit the little old church of San Fabiano, while the back streets and alleys which open unexpectedly behind the Piazza Marconi are absolutely fascinating. There is one old house called the Casa del Moretto (the House of the Little Moor) which we never succeeded in finding; while another ancient building, standing all by itself where two lanes meet, we found only to lose again. My plea to sacrifice luncheon in order to continue our search almost led to a domestic upheaval, but we have since wondered whether the two houses are one and the same.

We decided that Intra is a good place – especially on a Saturday morning, for Saturday is market day and Intra market is famous. There you can buy glass, china, dress-lengths, cheap jewellery, pottery from Laveno, and baskets – including those long, conical receptacles called *gherle* which peasants carry on their backs. *Gherle* are very rare nowadays, except in the mountain villages, but we did see a few.

The stalls display every kind of foodstuff; spaghetti, vermicelli – in fact, macaroni in all its forms, pasta, pizza, eggs, and every kind of exotic cheese, including that delicious pale gorgonzola which tastes so very different in Italy. For a few small coins you can buy a bouquet which will melt the hardest female heart, or enough little grapes to last you for days – and very sweet little grapes they are too. Or, standing under the portico of the Municipio, where are inscribed the names of those brave men of Intra who died under Garibaldi, you can watch their descendants laughing, quarrelling, haggling, gesticulating – buying a kilo of figs or oranges and acting every word of it in vivid pantomime. A market day in Intra is a sight for the gods, but you will have to get up early, for it is in full swing by eight o'clock.

Going north from the Gulf of Pallanza, you come to Ghiffa, where you have a distant view of the mighty peaks which mount guard over the Simplon. It is a pleasant little resort of scattered houses clustering round an ancient fortress – the Castello di Frino. Beyond it lies the rock village of Oggiogno where, in the fifteenth-century oratory of Cadessino on the hillside there are some interesting frescoes; and, continuing farther north still, just before you reach the glassworks of Porto Valtravaglia, you will see the Rocca di Caldè – a tenth-century stronghold of the Marquesses of Ivrea, which was destroyed by the Swiss in 1518. Indeed, you will notice that on this western shore, as the mountains close in, there are more castles and Maggiore begins to bear some resemblance to Lake Garda, where the Scaligeri of Verona left their mark in curtain-walls and towers.

And now you have reached the widest part of the Lake, between Cannèro and Luino – a district renowned, even in Italy, for its mild climate and the fertility of its soil. This part of the western shore is known as the Cannèro Riviera, for within easy reach of the town there are a number of small resorts in pleasant rural surroundings. And here it is time to call another halt, for Cannèro itself, among its olives and vineyards at the foot of Monte Carza, has much to offer the curious traveller with a taste for romance. Yet perhaps 'romance' is the wrong word, for its chief interest lies in two castles on islets, a short distance from the shore. They are not easy to see from a boat, for they blend into the background; but in the fifteenth century, the Castelli di Cannèro – or the Castelli di Malpaga, to give their more sinister name to robbers' dens built by forced labour – were held by the five Mazzardi brothers who, in a competition for sheer wickedness, would certainly have won a prize.

They look so pleasant and peaceful, those grey, towered ruins reflected in the water; but, from all accounts, things went on inside which are best left to the imagination. For 11 years, while Italy was rent by the wars between Guelph and Ghibelline – that is to say, the adherents of the Pope and the Holy Roman Emperor – those picturesque castles which are so photogenic and which made such charming studies for Victorian young ladies' sketch-books, were the centre of a reign of terror along the beautiful shores of Maggiore. No man's life and no woman's honour was safe from the five Mazzardi brothers, whose cold-blooded ferocity, utter ruthlessness and lust made them feared from Locarno to Sesto Calende until at last, in 1414, Duke Filippo Visconti of Milan marched against them with a small army. Even then it took a six-month's siege to breach their walls and bring the five villains to justice. A hundred years later, Lucovico Borromeo built a villa on those ill-omened islets. He cannot have been superstitious, for the credulous would say that they are haunted ground.

Luino, on the eastern shore and opposite those ill-omened islands, is another industrial town, at the mouths of the rivers Tresa and Magoràbbia. At one time it belonged to Switzerland; but, in the sixteenth century, the Swiss Confederacy exchanged it for Chiasso and Balerna. There is not a great deal to see there, but it is a pleasant place with plenty of entertainment and it is a good centre for exploring the northern end of the Lake. Bernadino Luini, the painter, was born in the town and some of his frescoes are to be seen in the church. The Town Hall is a sixteenth-century palace and near the landing-stage you will see the inevitable statue of Garibaldi. Indomitable as ever, after the first defeat of the Piedmontese at Custozza in 1848, he raised another gallant little army of 1,500 men and marched out of this town to renew the struggle against all the might of the

Hapsburgs. But, as I have said, Luino is mainly industrial nowadays. It has important silk factories and is easily accessible to the St Gotthard railway junction at Bellinzona.

Back on the western shore, in the northern reaches where the Lake is at its narrowest, another town of considerable interest though little visited is Cannóbio. Here again we have an industrial town which is also a holiday resort, but it should on no account be missed. I can see no reason why Cannóbio should not become very popular. With its ancient towers, its tortuous streets, its arches and old stone houses with outside stairs, it seemed to us one of the most picturesque places on Lake Maggiore. And – again on Saturdays – it has a most fascinating market, which extends all along the waterfront. Kay, I remember, bought quite a good cameo there, comparatively cheaply. But then the North Italian Lakes are famous for their cameos.

A massive granite Town Hall with cool arcades is, for some reason, called Il Paradiso; and a sculptured lion on the low cliff about half a mile from the landing-stage commemorates (if that is the word) the bombardment by Austrian warships in 1859. Cannóbio is the Maggiore base of the fast motor-launches of the Italian Preventive Service for, as always on a frontier, smuggling is a problem and the *doganieri* are busy men.

In a little piazza in which stands a fine old church, we watched the town band – a good one – muster and march away to take part in some function; and then discovered that the church was none other than that of the Madonna del Pietà, a place of great interest to Roman Catholics – so much so, indeed, that it could almost be called a pilgrimage church. We had both been so attracted by its story that we could not resist going in.

It is an impressive Renaissance building in the style of Bramante, with a dome by Pelegrino Tibaldi of Bologna and a façade of Baveno marble, while we found the interior even richer than we had expected – gradually changing from silver to gold as one approaches the High Altar. But for the faithful, the whole church is a shrine for a small picture of Christ on the Cross, between the Virgin Mary and St John.

Until the year 1522, this picture hung in a house down by the shore. But then the amazing story went round that, in some crisis or moment of tension, the painted figure of Our Saviour had exuded real blood. Very soon the house had been demolished and a little chapel built on the site to enshrine the picture more fittingly. The escape of Cannòbia from the Plague which, in the following year, devastated the countryside, was attributed to its influence; and 50 years later, the great Archbishop, Carlo Borromeo (of whom we shall have more to say when we reach Arona) decreed that the miraculous portrait should be encased in silver and housed in a more suitable setting. So the church of Madonna del Pietà began to arise, and certainly Cannòbia was left unscathed by further attacks of the pestilence in 1575 and 1623.

The sacred picture, heavily enshrined in silver, now has a place of honour on the High Altar, for the good people of the town have not forgotten their deliverance. Every year, on 8 January, the anniversary of the miracle, there are illuminations on the Lake; and on the evening of Whit Monday, in solemn procession, the Pietà is carried to the parish church of San Vittore. To the sound of music and chanting, and in a swirling cloud of incense, it is borne reverently through the streets, attended by the clergy of sixteen parishes, in their richest vestments, by bearers of banners and reliquaries, and by a guard of the local Carabinieri in their full-dress uniforms and plumed bicornes. It is a wonderful sight; and even those of us who are not Roman Catholics can hardly fail to be impressed by a demonstration of gratitude which is as deep and strong as ever after 400 years.

Continuing northwards along the Piedmontese shore towards Locarno, we soon cross into Switzerland. The torrent of Valmarra, which marks the frontier, is said to be the scene of a brisk traffic – both legal and illegal – for the near-by town of Brissago is chiefly remarkable for a large tobacco factory which helps to make life interesting for the Customs officers on both sides of the Border. The church is ringed by a grove of dark cypress trees, and, just off the shore, there are two beautiful islands called the Isole di Brissago.

Still farther north is the pleasant little resort of Ascona, an old town on the south-western side of the delta of the Maggia – another of those rivers which feed the great lake. I have heard that there are people who speak, not of Maggiore but of Lake Locarno; but it is not a practice that I recommend – at any rate, south of the Border. The Italians are a fiery people and inclined to be touchy about frontiers.

Situated at the foot of the mountains, Locarno is one of the most interesting towns in Switzerland. With Lugano and Bellinzona, it used to take its turn as capital of the Canton of Ticino, but it became internationally famous in 1925, when the Pact of Locarno settled the vexed question of the Rhineland and guaranteed the existing frontiers of France, Belgium and Germany. It retains all the characteristics of an Italian town and has only been Swiss since the sixteenth century. Before that it formed part of the Duchy of Milan and, earlier still, it belonged to the Bishop of Como.

Apart from its importance as a business centre, Locarno is a residential and health resort of outstanding beauty, the shore being gay with camellias, magnolia and mimosa. There are excellent facilities for all kinds of sport, including sailing, swimming, and skiing in the foothills of the Alps.

Dividing the town in two from east to west is the wide street and market called the Piazza Grande. There, in the public gardens, you will find the Kursaal Theatre, the Post Office and the Museum. It extends the whole length of the town, terminating in a ruined castle of the Visconti, begun in 1342 and sacked by the Swiss in 1512. Later, that part of the stronghold which remained habitable became the seat of the Swiss Bailiffs, and also a prison and a school of art. In one of the corridors there is a mural by Luini.

To the south of the Piazza Grande is the modern residential quarter. Houses and villas in their gardens, some of them very beautiful, reach as far as the wood called the Bosco dell' Isolino, while to the north of the main artery you will find the Old Town of narrow streets, cool arcades, and picturesque houses. To those who like exploring old churches I would recommend the parish church of Sant' Antonio, the cemetery chapel of Santa Maria in Selva, where there are the remains of fifteenth-century frescoes, and the secularized church of San Francesco. In the suburb of Muralto is the twelfth-century church of San Vittore; and if you go down into the crypt and examine the pillars, you will see some interesting sculptured capitals.

The principal sight in Locarno, however, is undoubtedly the complex of buildings which crowns a precipitous rock behind the west end of the town; and if, like us, you are lovers of fine scenery, you should visit this Franciscan monastery and pilgrimage church of Madonna del Sasso, built in 1480. If you are energetic and follow the old winding 'Way of the Chapels' upwards through the trees, it will take you about half an hour. Although it is shady, it is very steep, but there is a funicular which will get you to the top in 10 minutes with enough breath left in your body for you to enjoy the prospect that awaits you.

The approach to the church is through an open gallery or loggia with a bird's-eye view of the Lake. There are a number of groups of statuary in terracotta, and the church contains two notable pictures – 'The Flight into Egypt' by Bramante and 'The Entombment' by Antonio Ciseri. From this stage the funicular continues upwards to the little chapel of Santa Trinità dei Monti, and from here the views are magnificent. At your leisure and refreshed (for the terminus is blessed with a restaurant) you can see a great stretch of northern Maggiore. From this height it looks like a sheet of shining glass dotted with toy boats, a panorama of Alpine peaks bounds the view to the north, and, on either side of the town, are the deltas of the Maggia and Ticino rivers – the latter an old acquaintance of ours.

On your journey back to Pallanza you are faced with a choice. From Locarno you can either return to your base by boat, or, if you are travelling by car, you can take the road which runs along the eastern shore to Laveno. There is not much to see except the beauty of nature, but surely that should content anyone: the ruffled blue of the water, the mountains, the orchards and vineyards. And, talking of vineyards, did you ever hear the origin of the Garibaldi biscuit – that yellow confection filled with currants which we used to call 'squashed flies'? The story goes that Garibaldi's men, hard pressed and short of rations, were served out with biscuits harder, thicker, and even more unappetizing that anything known to the British Army in the First World War; and that on the march – perhaps even hereabouts, they used to buy or be given handfuls of raisins (if they were caught stealing them they were shot) and make a sort of primitive sandwich. Hence the name.

Zenna (Swiss) and Pino (Italian) need not detain you; and I do not think that you will want to stay long at the twin villages of Maccagno Superiore and Maccagno Inferiore on either side of the Giona, the river which waters the Valle Vedasco. But high on the hill above the last-named there is an ancient watch-tower and a picturesque old building called the Santuario della Madonna. You are driving now through the narrow Neck of the Lake; but soon the mountains fall back, the view opens out, and you have a clear run to Laveno and the car-ferry which will, I hope, bring you to your hotel in good time for a drink before dinner.

The Southern Arm

To describe the sinuous curves of the Italian Lakes is extremely difficult: with some of them, like Lake Lugano, it is almost impossible. That is why I suggested that you should make your base, as Kay and I usually do, at some central point and from there branch out in different directions. From Pallanza you have now seen both shores of the northern arm as far as Locarno at the head of the Lake, and you should now follow the southern arm which curves away to Sesto Calende in the south-east.

The best way to begin this new sortie is to go to Intra and

return on the ferry to Laveno. Before, you will remember, you went south from there by boat to see the rock church of Santa Caterina; but now you will probably prefer to continue southwards by road to that old, old church of San Donato, which is known locally as La Badia – the Abbey. Dating from the ninth century, it was originally the church of a Benedictine brotherhood, but there are later additions.The building has three naves, and pillars of red stone with Romanesque capitals, while on one side of it is a high campanile which is a landmark for miles. In Italy churches mean frescoes, and San Donato possesses several which you should find rewarding. In an apsidal chapel there is a 'Christ in Majesty' thought to date from the twelfth century: others were painted during the Renaissance and are by such artists as Tarilli, Zenalli, and Belotti.

By taking the turning to the right, you now come to the town of Angera, with its grim old Rocca rising on a hill to the north and commanding the narrows formed by the headland on which castle and town were built. Angera itself is a quiet residential town and holiday centre; but, if you are interested in medieval military architecture, you should drive up to the castle, which is one of the sights of Maggiore. Or, if you have no alternative – walk, as we did. It is hard work but it is worth it.

It so happened that, on the day I have in mind, Kay and I were carless. The winding road up the hill to the castle is longer, steeper, and even more tiring than it looks. And it was a hot afternoon. A very hot afternoon. But the guardians of the gates of Angera know all about weary wayfarers. As well as picture postcards, lemonade, ices and so forth, they sell enormous bottles of lager – the very largest bottles of lager that I have ever seen. It will be long before I forget them. Even now, if I close my eyes, I can feel that glorious beverage trickling and gurgling down my dry throat, changing my whole outlook on life as if it were, in very truth, the milk of human kindness. For a short time, under its influence, I loved my fellow-men.

There was a fortress here on this vantage-point in the time of the Lombards – that is to say, from the sixth century until

300 years later, when Charlemagne the Frank had himself crowned with the Iron Crown of Lombardy. Later, in the early thirteenth century, the ducal house of Visconti built a castle on the same site and took the additional title of Counts of Angera. For a time the stronghold came into the possession of the Archbishop of Milan, and in the fifteenth century it passed to the powerful family of Borromeo. So, as in course of time, the need for strong defences became less acute, various alterations were made, which turned the old *rocca* into a veritable palace. But there is still much of the old to be seen.

Entrance is through fortified outer and inner gateways, past the guardhouse and into the courtyard, dominated by the tall Maschio Tower – the Italian equivalent of a keep. In the Hall of Justice there are frescoes dating from the fourteenth century, when the Visconti of Milan held sway; but in the sixteenth and seventeeth centuries extensive alterations were made, mostly on the western side of the huge courtyard, and these later rooms are now a treasury of furniture and pictures.

I have spoken of the Borromeï – lords of the Castle of Angera, whose old and honoured name still resounds from end to end of Maggiore. If you look across the water to Arona on the western shore, you will see on a hill just outside the town something that looks like a tall pillar. This is a colossal statue to the most famous member of the family, San Carlo Borromeo. You must have a closer look at it later.

In the meantime, returning to the main road, you should (if you are travelling by car) head south for Sesto Calende. It is set in flat land at the foot of the Lake, green and well-watered; and there, bright blue now and navigable on its way to join the Po, you will meet the Ticino river again, which you last observed entering the Lake at Locarno. The snow-clad Alps are still visible, far away on the northern horizon; but I do not think that you will want to remain long among the factories and offices of this industrial town – unless you are ready for a swim after your long drive, for there is an excellent beach.

Sesto Calende, by the way – although it is doubtful if you

would ever suspect it – is a place of considerable antiquity. A number of pre-Roman tombs have been found in the neighbourhood and the name itself is derived from the Roman market which was held on the sixth day before the Calends, the Calends being the first day of the month. Alternatively, you could have reached Sesto Calende by steamer from Laveno.

Rounding the southern end of the Lake, the first place of interest to which you will come is Arona on the western shore. It is an ancient town which is still of considerable importance, being a railway junction of lines to the Alpine passes and to Milan, Turin and Genoa. It is also a terminus for the Lake steamers and hydrofoils. Unfortunately, as is so often the case nowadays, the picturesque waterfront that Ruskin knew has been marred by characterless modern buildings such as can be seen anywhere from the Costa Brava to Miami: from a distance they look about as interesting as a set of dominoes standing on end. I suppose that, one day, the phase will pass and that architects will cease to be inspired by honeycombs and match-boxes. In the meantime, if you approach Arona by boat, you must just grit your teeth, avert your eyes from this trendy façade, and make your way to the back streets where you can still find Italy.

There are some interesting old churches, and in them the pictures that one has come to expect in this part of Europe. In Santa Martiri, a Gothic building, there are a number of minor masterpieces – among them an altar-piece by Bergogni; and this church also contains a reliquary to SS Fedele and Carpóforo, a lovely thing made of crystal. Then, in the collegiate church of Santa Maria, the Borromeo Chapel has an altar-piece which is a polyptych painted by Gaudenzio Ferrari in 1511, the six panels depicting the Eternal Father, the Holy Family, eight saints, and the Countess Borromeo. This lady was the donor.

Arona *is* the Borromeï: it is as difficult to escape from them as it is from Prince Charlie in the Highlands. Not that one would wish to do so, for the influence of the former lords of Angera was, in the main, beneficial, as witness many acts of charity and the foundation of the great Ambrosian Library at Milan; and even in these democratic days, the Borromeï are greatly respected. The only bone that I have to pick with this illustrious family is that I don't like the huge bronze statue of their famous ancestor – the colossus – some would say, the monstrosity – which looms over the countryside from a hill just outside the town; and I am not sure that I would not find that some of the Borromeï agreed with me.

Do you remember that pillar which I pointed out to you from the other side of the Lake at Angera? Well, now the time has come for you to make its closer acquaintance and for me to tell you just a little of the long story of the Borromeï which, ever since the Middle Ages, has been a name to conjure with on the Italian Lakes. I understand that the present head of the house, Prince Borromeo, lives in Milan but that he spends some time each year at his palace on Isola Bella.

The family has given the world many great men and one saint – San Carlo Borromeo. Born at Arona in 1538, in a castle which is now in ruins, he was given a cardinal's hat at the age of 22 by his uncle, Pope Pius IV. Appointed to the vacant see of Milan in 1563, only then was he ordained priest and made – first a bishop and, then, a year later, Archbishop of Milan. Nowadays we would call it a flagrant case of nepotism; but Carlo Borromeo was a dedicated son of the Church and there is no reason to suppose that she ever regretted his elevation. For one thing, he was a notable persecutor of heretics (which, in his time, was considered a virtue) and he even wrote a letter complaining that there were not enough executions.

But this was the sixteenth century and it is not fair to judge him by modern standards. Let me hasten to add that there was a more attractive side to his character. Although he is usually remembered as a stern disciplinarian and reformer, he is even more famous for his selflessness and heroism in time of plague. To his own clergy he set an example of austere and virtuous living; he endowed schools and seminaries, and was unwearying in his work for the poor. He had his enemies who tried in vain to bring about his downfall and there was even an attempt to assassinate him by members of a religious order called the Humiliati. But he prevailed against them all, died peacefully in 1584, and was canonized only 26 years later.

And how did posterity reward this saintly ascetic? One of his own family caused this monstrous statue of bronze and lead to be erected in his honour. With its pedestal of granite, it is 105 feet or about 31 metres high; it is known locally as San Carlone, and it is an eyesore for miles. Those of you who are statistically minded may be interested to hear that the head measures 6.50 metres or about seven yards, and that the thumb is about one metre or one yard in length. For a small fee visitors are allowed to climb a series of ladders inside the colossus – though what satisfaction they get from doing so is quite beyond me. I have been told that on a hot day you are almost roasted alive in the brazen inferno which is the giant's head or, alternatively, you can come to an even more messy end by slipping while passing from one ladder to another. I do not know whether there has ever been a fatal accident but, until recently, the authorities wisely banned the exploration of San Carlone's interior.

If, after leaving Arona, you continue by road up the western shore, your next port of call is Stresa, but you will be well advised to stop at several smaller places on the way. The impression left by Meina is of a succession of parks and gardens, culminating in the magnificent grounds of the Villa Faraggiana. And after that, if you have time, you should venture a short distance inland to the mountain hamlet of Massino, where there is a church, a castle, and – at a height of 2,656 feet (800 metres) – the deserted chapel of San Salvatore. At one time it was a hermitage, and from it there are wonderful views across the Lake towards Varese and Como.

Next you will come to Lesa and Belgirate, which nowadays are one continuous town. You may not be tempted to stay long

3 *Brissago on Lake Maggiore*

in Lesa, which is mainly industrial, manufacturing cotton, woollen goods and paper; but there is another view – from the headland by Belgirate – which has been described as one of the noblest on Lake Maggiore.

You will find an even grander view at Stresa, but Belgirate has places of interest for those to whom the past can give as much pleasure as the present. Another ruined castle, a Renaissance church, and a villa once occupied by Josephine, the wife of Napoleon, and the little town was once the scene of a most poignant tragedy, for here lived the widow Adelaide, better known 100 years ago as 'the mother of the Cairoli'. She had five sons and she sacrificed four of them in the War of Liberation. They were Garibaldini and, like their dead father and the only surviving son, Benedetto Cairolo the statesman, had shown all Italy an example of patriotism and integrity – old-fashioned virtues at which, in our enlightened age, intellectuals have been known to sneer.

As a centre for Lake Maggiore, Stresa – or Stresa Borromeo, to give the town its official name – rivals its neighbours, Baveno and Pallanza, on the other side of the Gulf. Some people even prefer it. Its situation is incomparable; and certainly it is a beautiful place in its modern way, with great hotels – in one of which we had a most expensive tea – white villas and lush gardens mirrored in the clear water. But, like Arona, it might be anywhere: to us, at any rate, its atmosphere is international, not Italian. On the other hand, it has little to show of historical interest; and, knowing myself, that may well be the reason why I prefer its rivals. If you have only a short time there, my advice is not to linger on the front, which is like the front of any other smart watering-place, but to wander at random up the back streets. They are not as interesting as those of Pallanza and Intra, but they are quite attractive. Kay shares my views but I think that, perhaps, her taste is more catholic than mine.

Stresa, like Baveno, is an excellent jumping-off ground for Lake Orta, and – even more than Pallanza – is ideal for visiting

4 *Lakeside promenade, Como*

the fabulous Borromean Islands which, as first seen across the water, seem almost too beautiful for this world – a dream of white marble, red roofs, and gardens, reflected in the still water. And Stresa has another advantage. It lies at the foot of Monte Mottarone and is not only a famous centre for winter sports but offers a fine field of action for climbers and walkers. The ascent of the mountain (4,890 feet or 1,500 metres) is not difficult; but for those who love their ease as I do nowadays, there is a funicular.

The views from the summit are magnificent: it is said that, on a clear day, you can see Milan Cathedral. You can certainly expect a panorama of the Alps, the wide sweep of the Plain of Lombardy, glimpses of seven lakes, and, in the far north by Locarno, twin ribbons of silver, one of which is our old friend the Ticino River which always brings back memories of the days when we followed it down from the mountains.

On the outskirts of the town, as you approach from Belgirate, there are two houses of beauty and interest: the Villa Pallavicini and the Villa Vignola; while adjoining the church on the rising ground to the south-east, is the Villa Ducale, once the home of the Duchess of Genoa, Mother of Queen Margherita. Earlier, it belonged to Antonio Rosmini-Serbati, priest and philosopher (1797–1855) whose voluminous and controversial works earned him, first, the approval and then the censure of the Vatican. Towards the end of his stormy career, he retired to this house in Stresa, which is now the Collegio Rosmini and the property of a charitable order founded by the great philosopher. In the church you can see his monument by the sculptor Vela.

Baveno, famous for its granite and marble quarries, is a popular resort on the south shore of the Gulf of Pallanza. Any aerial photograph shows very clearly that it is a green place, a town of terraced gardens – even compared with Pallanza and Stresa. And here again, like the other two towns, it has its champions who are prepared to swear that Baveno is the best of all centres from which to explore Lake Maggiore. There are first-rate hotels and many delightful villas half-hidden among trees; and there is also the Castello Branco, which can hardly be called delightful, for its English style sticks out like a sore thumb in its Italian setting. But it should be very dear to our countrymen, for it had the honour of being the holiday residence of Queen Victoria. Then you should see the parish church of SS Gervasio and Protasio which, with the near-by Baptistry, dates from the eleventh and twelfth centuries and still retains traces of that Romanesque period which in our own country we call Norman. There are some interesting frescoes.

A modern, civilized resort and still unspoiled. But the town of Baveno itself is not the whole story. As I have said, it is noted for its quarries of red and white marble, some of which was used in the building of Milan Cathedral. Like the inhabitants of our own Isle of Portland, the quarrymen are a race apart. The villages near Ferio, to the north of the town, are entirely devoted to the labour of these *scalpellini* or stone-cutters, and their yards and sheds on the shore of the Lake have transport at their very doorsteps.

Behind Baveno and Stresa, and separating the basin of Lake Maggiore from that of Lake Orta, rises the mountain ridge called Mergozzolo, of which the highest peak is Mottarone. It is not well known – a rather mysterious district, seldom visited by foreigners. There is, or was until recently, little intercourse between the mountaineers and the people who live in the towns on the Gulf. The former are said to be strange, secretive folk who prefer the old ways, and harbour beliefs and superstitions which go back to the days of the Lombards. A queer little pocket of ancient lore surviving in modern Italy. I have not been there myself, but it was in these mountains that the legends of the werewolves of the Lake originated, with gruesome tales of benighted travellers and uncanny metamorphoses. Does witchcraft still flourish there? Sometimes I wonder. No doubt Radio and the motor-car have brought many changes to these remote hamlets. Modern Science may have banished Ancient Evil. It may well be so. But I would not bet on it.

The Borromean Islands

In Victorian times – and, presumably, after the long War of Liberation had ended – it used to be said the Borromean Islands were the ideal place for a honeymoon. Edwin visualized dearest Angelina languishing under the cypress trees, while she longed to see those golden whiskers reflected in a lily-pool. It has also been said, perhaps with some truth, that it is wiser to keep a certain distance between you and those islands of enchantment. Then you will board the aircraft at Milan quite certain that, for all your sins, you have been vouchsafed a glimpse of Paradise. I can answer for this. More years ago than I care to remember, I saw the islands for the first time from a train on its way to Florence. Through all the ups and downs of life, through marriage and war and the run of years, I have cherished that beautiful vision. It was only comparatively recently that I set foot on the islands, and then I came away slightly – ever so slightly – disillusioned.

There are really five Borromean Islands; but two of them, La Marghera and San Giovanni, are too small to be of much interest and, in any case, visitors are not allowed to land. San Giovanni lies so close to the mainland that it almost forms part of the Punta della Castagnola. In the Dark Ages this little island had its own church and was strongly fortified. But the glory has departed.

Your first visit will probably be to Isola Madre, the largest of the three main islands and the nearest to Pallanza. But if you are in a hurry, do not attempt it, for the island is private property and, once inside the wrought iron gates, you are supposed to remain with an escorted tour – something that Kay and I particularly detest. I am prepared to admit that, with plant-thieves and vandals on the loose, this precaution is necessary. But we could not face the ordeal. We escaped, and – with many apologies – I must confess that all I can tell you about Isola Madre is by heresay.

The whole place is really one huge botanical garden, in the middle of which is a piazza shaded by a huge cypress, and the eighteenth-century villa which belongs to the ancient family that still owns all but one of the islands and which gave them their name. In the beautifully laid-out grounds, traversed by shady avenues, are semi-tropical shrubs and flowers growing in such colourful profusion that they fill the hearts of all gardeners who see them with envy. There are pools and fountains; stately white peacocks stalk through the shadows like pale ghosts, while through gaps in great masses of camellia, oleander and bouganvillæa, you can catch glimpses of the mainland: houses and hotels, clear-cut as strings of beads – ivory and amber, or shimmering in the heat-haze as they rise, tier upon tier, towards the foothills of the mountains.

Your next port of call will almost certainly be Isola dei Pescatori – the Fishermen's Island. It is independent, unspoiled, and a complete contrast to Isola Madre. One of the most picturesque places on Maggiore, it is said to be especially appealing to writers and artists. This is true. I dislike the word 'quaint' but I cannot think of a better one with which to describe this fishing-village. There is only one cobbled street, with side-lanes leading down to the shore. Iron balconies are gay with flowers and the houses are packed so closely together that it is difficult to imagine how they fitted in the last one. And along by the edge of the water are vociferous stall-holders selling souvenirs to tourists. But if ever commercialization can be forgiven, it is here, for the stalls are bright with crude, primary colours and make the street as gay as a garden.

At the southern end of the long, narrow island, the fishermen's church of San Vittore, unlike many Italian churches, is light and airy, with some remarkably beautiful silver candlesticks on the altar; but the northern end tapers into a triangular grass-grown 'piazza', rather like the prow of a ship, and the only open space on the island. Here you can stroll or lounge on the seats under the trees, and here you can see the moored *luciè* with their brightly coloured awnings vivid against the sparkling water. There are little cafés and wineshops (just the sort I like) where you can dally over an ice or a drink as you watch the local inhabitants going about their business – and also, unfortunately, the crowds of visitors going about theirs. But I had better hurriedly change the subject, for we were visitors ourselves – something that occasionally one is apt to forget.

I sometimes wonder what this little self-contained community would be like in the winter. Given a good knowledge of Italian, to stay there could be quite an experience, for you would see the real thing and not just a swarm of foreigners buying picture postcards. The views from the island are superb: Baveno and the mountains behind it, the great gashes made by the quarries and, far away, Monte Orfano and the Corno di Nibbo.

You have nearly finished your tour of the Borromean Islands and, indeed, of Maggiore itself. But before you leave for Lake Como, there is that 'must' with the beautiful name. The fairy isle. The earthly paradise. The tourist trap. Isola Bella. It was the creation of a man with a great idea, a noble ambition – to take a barren rock and make it blossom in honour of the wife he adored. And although some of us cold northerners may sneer loftily at what we like to pretend is gross extravagance – mere bravura, how many of us would not give a lot to be able to do the same!

Isola Bella does not, as many believe, mean the Beautiful Island but is, rather, a play on a woman's name, which happened to be Isabella. The authorities differ as to the exact date; but it was about the middle of the seventeenth century when Count Carlo Borromeo had his splendid inspiration, began to import soil from the mainland, and pile it up into a great hill on the top of which he planned to build his house. Unfortunately he died before this ambitious project could be completed, but the work was carried on by his dutiful son, Vitaliano.

You land from the steamer at a stone quay; and from there a village street runs uphill, past the church, to the gates of the palace. The estate consists of 10 balustraded terraces, mounting from the edge of the Lake to the Palazzo Borromeo itself which, although the visitor would never suspect it, remains unfinished. The construction must have been a colossal task and enough to tax the ingenuity of even this nation of gardeners. And did the Borromeï succeed? In many ways, I would say, yes – though I doubt if these gardens are as impressive as the older and much simpler grounds of Isola Madre.

And here, in spite of what I have said, I must be allowed a few words of criticism. Those who indulge in cheap sneers at certain aspects of Isola Bella may be guilty of bad manners but they certainly have a case. The gardens, wonderful as they are, are in places too flamboyant, too ornate: they provoke the wrong kind of comment, for they culminate in the Unicorn Terrace and that really is a little too much. It is so overcrowded with dubious statuary that, to the irreverent, it looks like something between a roundabout and a wedding-cake. Crowded into a comparatively small space there are urns, obelisks, grottos, a ramping unicorn (badge of the Borromeï) and a lot of little cherubs apparently dancing the Highland Fling.

Even here, of course, it is possible to be carried away by the sheer lavishness and exuberance of the whole conception. Better judges have praised and been enchanted by the Unicorn Terrace. But, for my part, I felt slightly dazed and so did Kay, so we moved on rapidly to admire the rest of the garden – which was easy, for most of it is really beautiful. We found the same glimpses of green water framed in sagging branches that, I am told, is one of the features of Isola Madre – though perhaps Isola Bella is not quite so luxuriant. I cannot tell. But there are orange and lemon trees, ilex, camphor and cedar, solemn cypresses, myrtle, hybiscus, immaculate flights of steps, patterned flower-beds, shady pools of water-lilies; there are white doves and white, rather supercilious-looking peacocks. If you can forget the one false note struck by that prancing unicorn, you will remember a seventeenth-century Italian garden at its best.

At Isola Bella you see the house before you go out into the

gardens, but I have left the palace until last because, to us, it was the 'clou': it should have been the grand climax. It is a princely mansion, worthy of the men who made it. Moreover, you are allowed to wander freely. There are no irritating restrictions, no incomprehensible guides herding tourists like sheep.

You enter the palace through a small ante-chamber – or perhaps I should say guard-room, for the walls are hung with the helmets, corselets and halberds with which the seventeenth-century Borromeï armed their retainers. And, then, one by one, you pass through some of the most magnificent apartments that we have ever seen. Perhaps the best is the first that you see – the Great Hall. It is decorated in the palest eggshell blue and white, ornate but not overwhelmingly so, and perfectly proportioned. Like the other rooms, it has a vast marble floor, most intricately patterned – a floor that gleams and calls for the lightest of pumps: in modern shoes you feel clumsy. Then there is the Ballroom, with walls lined with mirrors which must have multiplied the shifting kaleidoscope of dancers a hundredfold; the room in which Napoleon slept – pale pink with a big red four-poster; the Room of the Medals; the Main Staircase of the Armorial Bearings – and, in all of them, floors so beautiful that we almost forget to look at the surroundings. Yet, when she could spare a glance from the marble, Kay told me that the colour and design of some of the tapestried furniture were almost beyond praise. There were other tapestries too – great Gobelin hangings, porcelain and pictures, including a number of Old Masters, some of which have been on loan to Hampton Court Palace.

And then we went down to the basement and – to me, at least – the atmosphere changed. We walked through grottos of real and imitation shells, like artificial caverns; and in them were displayed wonderful sets of puppets and marionettes, each about a foot high. There were sixteenth-century Borromeï leaving their castle of Angera by coach, with their nobles, outriders and guards; there were ladies and gentlemen of the period, soldiers, Turks, leering devils, figures that looked like torturers, and ghastly skeletons in Hell. I have always been foolishly susceptible to such things and somehow I did not care for those puppets. They were interesting, even fascinating, but they looked as if they might be endowed with a secret life of their own and that when the great doors of the palace had closed behind the last visitor, there might be strange doings down there in the grottos – perhaps the grim re-enactment of half-forgotten tragedies in miniature.

Whether or not you admire Isola Bella and the Palazzo Borromeo as much as we did, you can hardly deny that those who conceived and planned it 'thought big' – to use an ugly phrase which they would have despised. For love of his lady, Count Borromeo wrought a minor miracle when he gave orders that turned a barren rock into a garden crowned by a palace which is the apotheosis of wealth, opulence, and lordly splendour.

2. Lake Como

The Centro Lario

Como, the Lacus Larius of the Romans, has been described as 'the most romantic lake in the world'. Smaller than either Maggiore or Garda – some 31 miles long and $2\frac{1}{2}$ miles across at its widest point, just north of Bellagio (50 km × 4 km). I would not be far wrong in saying that it is the most famous of them all. As for its shape, it may help a little if I ask you to imagine an inverted 'Y' – Y. Then the up-stroke or most northerly arm leads to Colico; the south-easterly leads to Lecco; and the south-westerly and most beautiful arm to the ancient city of Como. At the Centro Lario, as it is called, where the three branches meet, is Bellagio; and here, on our last visit, Kay and I made our headquarters, for this central position gives one freedom to explore the whole lake – either by the steamers which ply from point to point, or by the great motor-road which encircles it.

Maggiore and Como are very different. The former is more open and spacious, the mountains rising farther back from the shore, while Como is a narrow lake enclosed by steep mountain walls. In both cases the brilliance of the colouring has to be seen to be believed; but, for some subtle reason which it is difficult to define, the Larian Lake possesses a softer, more voluptuous charm than its neighbours. Somehow it seems more attuned to the chirruping *grilli* and the song of the nightingale in the warm dusk. There are many – very many – to whom Lake Como is a paradise, with its luxurious villas drowsing on the edge of the sparkling water, its warm perfumed air, its lush semi-tropical gardens, and its long vistas backed by the Alpine peaks on the horizon. In the noonday heat or in the white moonlight it will give you unforgettable memories.

There is just one thing, however, which should be stated quite clearly. The people who compile travel brochures and the writers of seedsmen's catalogues are horses from the same stable. Both are blessed with a keen eye for colour and with eternal optimism. The promises of those who assure you that a small packet of seeds will produce a blaze of breath-taking beauty and those who predict blue water, bluer skies, and a riot of colour for all who visit the Italian Lakes should be taken with a large pinch of salt. Their descriptions are true but they are not true all the time. Como can look as cheerful as Clapham Junction on a wet Sunday afternoon. Kay and I have vivid memories of a journey by car to Bellagio from Pallanza on Lake Maggiore. It was in June but we drove through something resembling a Scotch mist, plus heavy rain and a rattle of hail on the roof of the car which sounded like machine-gun fire. Yet Italy can be a generous mistress to those who love her and sing her praises. While we ate our luncheon in the hotel at Bellagio, the storm-clouds rolled away across the mountains in a way that would have delighted the most sanguine of travel agents.

There is so much to enjoy that it should content you, for if, like us, you delight in the old, the picturesque, and all the colour and beauty which survives from the past, you may be lucky enough to witness one of those ancient ceremonies like the Blessing of the Lake, when priests in their gorgeous vestments go out by barge to cast a wreath upon the water; the September Festa Navale del Lario, in which feats of strength and skill recall bloody battles of the Middle Ages; or even the annual regatta, which is held at a different centre each year, while in two lonely villages in the Province of Como – Cavalleria and Inverigo – the national costume is still habitually worn – mostly, as I said before when we were on the shores of Maggiore, by elderly women who love the old ways. But if, on the other hand, having travelled all this way, you prefer to spend your time playing tennis, sailing, swimming, or merely basting yourself with sun-tan oil, let me assure you that Lake Como will give you every satisfaction. Old Lario has learned to be all things to all men – and women: up to the minute for the 'trendies', old-fashioned for those who like it that way. So many modes and manners have come and gone: they arise and ripple and disappear, like the little waves in the sunshine.

It is easy to reach the Lake – by air to Milan, or by road or rail over the St Gotthard Pass to the frontier town of Chiasso. From there you can travel to the City of Como by way of Lugano; but if you intend to stay at one of the northern resorts, you should leave the train at Lugano, as we once did, and make the rest of the journey by car, bus, or best of all by boat, to Porlezza. From Porlezza it is a pleasant drive past the little lake called Piano through the Val di Menaggio to the town of that name, and from there you can travel to any of the central or northern resorts by lake steamer. From Milan, on the other hand, it is an easy journey by road or rail to the city of Como. Here you leave the railway but there are plenty of steamers and there is a good road to Bellagio, where I hope you are going to stay.

Bellagio, 'Pearl of the Lake', as the Italians call it, is one of the loveliest and most popular resorts in Europe. An old Lombard town with its roots in the past, it has moved with the times, acquiring smart shops and hotels, and a promenade made beautiful by a long line of oleanders. But its steep, narrow streets still meander uphill towards the great wedge-shaped promontory which commands all three arms of the Lake, and from its campanili peal bells justly renowned for their sweetness of tone. To listen for the first time to the bells of Bellagio sounding across the still water is an experience for which any traveller is to be envied.

There are no supermarkets in these lakeland towns, but down on the waterfront and in the steep alleys there are some good shops, especially for such things as women's dresses, shoes and jewellery – and others which sell souvenirs and other profitable trash for tourists. There are also what I might call the *real* shops where the townspeople buy the necessities of life, including food and wine. We found them fascinating, with their straw-covered bottles, their oil and loaves and pasta, their many kinds of macaroni and sausages – and their cheese.

Mr H. V. Morton has praised gorgonzola as it is sold in Italy more eloquently than I can, but I paid my tribute to this noble cheese by bringing two pounds of it home to England. That cheese spoke for itself. When I explained the contents of my bag to the Customs officer at Milan Airport, he gave it one quick glance, his nose twitched, and he passed it without a word. But in the hot aircraft it wilted a little and I have an uneasy feeling that, as it did so, my popularity waned. At home in Sussex I enjoyed that cheese – or, rather, I enjoyed most of it. For one morning, while my back was turned, Kay hardened her heart, held her nose, and dropped the remains of my beautiful gorgonzola into the dustbin. When, at last, I learned of the betrayal our marriage was on the rocks for quite 10 minutes, and there are still moments when I mourn my fragrant souvenir of Bellagio.

I suppose one must concede that the town's principal industry today is tourism, but it is also well-known for its silk-weaving and for the skilful carving of olive-wood. And it has so much to offer the traveller. My advice is that when you first arrive and are comfortably settled in your hotel, you should find your way down to the quay and from there just wander up the hill, over the cobblestones – round and about at your pleasure. And, although I realize that it may not always be possible. Kay and I agree that, ideally, this little adventure should take place at night. One's first acquaintance with a strange town or village is always best made under cover of darkness when every pool of light is a mystery – or, better still, by moonshine, for then everything looks different and you can count on the exploration of quite a new town next morning.

In Bellagio there are two interesting churches. One, the parish church of San Giacomo, is in the heart of the Old Town and you will come to it if you follow the Via Garibaldi up from the harbour. In spite of much restoration, and the rebuilding of the upper half of the campanile 300 years ago, it is well worth a visit. It has three naves, each with its semi-circular apse, and boasts a fifteenth-century triptych, 'The Descent from the Cross' by Pietro Vannucci (Perugino), though, in spite of groups of flickering candles, it is too dark to see the picture properly. There is also a tiny disused church, 1,200 years old, in the Via Giuseppe Garibaldi. Unfortunately, it is bolted and barred.

We also liked the church of San Giovanni in the village of that name which, with Lóppia on the Como branch and other villages on the Lecco arm of the Lake, now form one continuous township with Bellagio – a double stretch of villas and gardens outlining a triangular wedge of which the apex is the promontory which commands the whole central basin.

Each, however, preserves its own character and individuality. Lóppia, a little island in a sea of sophistication, cannot have changed much in 100 years. In the tiny harbour we saw moored *luciè* with their coloured awnings and masts for the sails which, unfortunately, they no longer carry. And in the private grounds of the Villa Gerli there is a wonderful little Romanesque church with a low, loopholed belfry. There are wayside shrines which tell of a simple faith, and at the little *bottega* at San Giovanni where we stopped for a drink, the children of the proprietress were sent quite a long way to direct us to the church. It was an act of natural courtesy which we found very charming.

Here in San Giovanni there is a great painting by Gaudenzio Ferrara. It hangs on the south side of the church and portrays Christ in Glory, with St Peter and St Paul. The instruments of the Passion are borne aloft by flying angels, and the kneeling worshippers and witnesses are positively alive. But it is its bell which makes this little church so unforgettable, for among all the bells of this central area, San Giovanni's reigns supreme. Mellow and deep-throated, it can be heard for miles when it calls all good Catholics to prayer, dominating the lighter voices of the other churches.

For some distance beyond San Giovanni the mountains drop sheer down to the water, and for centuries this part of the Lake has been famous for the size of its fish. I have been told that 20-pound trout are not unusual, while there are old legends of 100-pounders and of scaly 'monsters' – fish or reptiles – which are said to have been seen on the shore. Perhaps they were like that dried horror which Kay and I once saw decorating the old gateway of Bregenz and which at some time must have emerged from the mysterious depths of Lake Constance.

I have spoken of villas and here, perhaps, a word of warning may be helpful. If he is wise, the visitor to the Lakes will exercise a certain discretion, a certain restraint, or – beautiful and interesting as they undoubtedly are – he may find that the villas, far from being a pleasure, will become a solemn duty, like the art galleries of Florence. Just as one tramps the miles (it seems miles!) of the Pitti Palace with aching feet and drunk with Old Masters, so it is possible to have a surfeit of statuary, however exquisite, and of avenues of cypress trees, however melancholy and romantic; and, confronted by yet another masterpiece of the Renaissance, to long for a simple Kentish manor or the warm glow of Cotswold stone. The villas of the Italian Lakes are among the great treasures of Europe. See them, enjoy them, but do not overdo it, and they will enrich your memories.

There are several of these noble houses in or near Bellagio: the Villa Trotti and the Villa Trivulzio at San Giovanni; the Villa Melzi, whose gardens are among the most famous in Italy and which contains a rarity – a self-portrait bust by Michelangelo; the Villa Poldi Pezzoli, in the grounds of which there is a Gonzaga mausoleum; and the Villa Giulia, which faces the Lecco arm of the Lake and which is renowned, even among its compeers, for the loveliness of its gardens. And yet, surely, that is no great compliment when they are all so beautiful – those wonderfully kept 'stately homes' of Italy, with their immaculate marble goddesses, their shaven lawns, their proud peacocks, and well-swept terraces. In a Bateman mood, one wonders what would happen to the unfortunate man who dropped a cigarette-end.

Above all, there are the Villa Carlotta, which can be seen across the water, and the Villa Serbelloni, now the property of the Rockefeller Foundation, in the grounds of which are the remains of medieval walls, and a small church which, in more dangerous days, was converted into a watch-tower.

And that brings me to one of the most interesting features of this place – the bold, almost awe-inspiring promontory called the Punta di Bellagio. It marks the end of the Brianza, that huge ridge of glacial debris which divides the Como from the Lecco arm of the Lake. Over 14 miles (24 km) wide at its base, the High Brianza is wooded and mountainous, and watered by a number of small lakes and tarns. Today there are houses, pink, white and yellow: there are villages and roads. But once it was a wilderness, notorious as a haunt of murderers and outlaws. The Romans tamed it and the Younger Pliny had a villa on 'this lofty ridge commanding two waters'; but in the wilder centuries that followed, when the legions had disintegrated and the Pax Romana was no more, robber lords built a stronghold on the promontory where Pliny's villa had stood. From there they levied toll on shipping and wreaked their wicked will on their neighbours. One charming lady, the Countess Borgomanero, was in the habit of disposing of discarded lovers by the simple expedient of having them thrown over the cliff, while the peaceful inhabitants of the lakeside, going about their lawful occasions, never left home in the morning without the very real fear that they might be knocked on the head before nightfall. Things reached such a pass that in 1375 Galeazzo Visconti, Duke of Milan, sent an expedition into no-man's-land and burned down the castle. But although the chief robbers' nest had been smoked out, there were still many refuges for criminals in the High Brianza, and law and order was little more than a hope for the future. As late as the closing years of the fifteenth-century, the

5 *Cadenabbia on Lake Como*

Marquis Stanga was granted permission by the Sforza to build himself a lordly villa on this dangerous ground, but he built too soon and his house was destroyed by a band of marauders from the Val Cavargna.

Yet even in Renaissance Italy such conditions could not last for ever. In the next century the barren rock was planted with trees; and in 1558, where the outlaws' stronghold had once stood, the Villa Serbelloni arose, with 800 steps leading down to the shore. Now there are gardens fragrant with roses and myrtle, and rich with pomegranates, citron and flowering shrubs, where little green lizards bask on the sun-baked stone and groves of umbrella pines cast a welcome shade. From this great height, as at Locarno, you can look down on a model railway, a miniature town, and tiny yachts gliding over a lake as smooth as satin – those dreamy, tranquil waters which yet, on occasion, can be lashed into fury by the two winds of Como: the Tivana, which comes sweeping down from the Alps, and the Brava which blows from south to north. Down below you, by the waterside, is the patial Hotel Villa Serbelloni.

The Lecco Arm

And now it is time to leave Bellagio and travel round the Lake. Let us begin with what some people think is the least interesting arm – a verdict with which I disagree. It runs south-east to Lecco town and is sometimes called the Lago di Lecco. Leaving it on our left, we can follow the road which skirts the eastern shore of the Brianza, but we shall find little to detain us except, perhaps, the village of Onno, Civenna with its twin campanili high on the hill-road, and Limonta – famous for the excellence of the chestnuts which grow so profusely in the hanging woods.

It may be asked why this side of the great upland ridge has so few villages and has, in consequence, so often been labelled uninteresting. Yet surely the answer is obvious. The Como arm of the Lake was protected by the ships and men-at-arms of that city; and, even when things were at their worst, it was possible

6 *Approaching Tremezzo, Lake Como*

to maintain some sort of law and order. But these eastern slopes of the High Brianza had no such advantage. All through the early Middle Ages this was cut-throat country, so there are few historical monuments. In this sort of 'debatable land', like our own Border Marches, there was little scope for the architect. If one built at all, it was for defence – or in such a simple fashion that it was easy for a house to arise, phoenix-like, from its ashes. One is reminded of Sir Walter Scott in grimly humorous mood:

They crossed the Liddel at curfew hour
And burned my little lonely tower;
The fiend receive their souls therefor!
It had not been burnt' this year or more –

But natural beauty can survive centuries of brigandage, and this is superb walking country. You can follow delightful lanes up through the vineyards and grey olive orchards to the groves of chestnut and walnut trees with, nearly all the time, glimpses of shining water through the intricate pattern of interlaced branches.

The ancient town of Lecco lies at the south-eastern end of the Lake, where it is drained by the River Adda, which entered it from the north. It has known Etruscans, Romans, Gauls, Lombards, and Austrians, and is now a flourishing manufacturing centre – a vast agglomeration of factories, office-blocks and high-rise flats, with a statue of Garibaldi looking rather out of place among all this modernity. At Lecco they produce iron, brass, copper and, above all, silk; and nowadays it has good communications by water, road and rail. Its station is on the Milan-Colico-Sondrio line.

The town lies in the shadow of Monte Resegone (6,152 feet or 1,923 m) – a rugged wall of bare granite, buttressed and fluted. Its grim saw-edge of granite peaks dominates the district, while to the south-west, rising alone by the little lake at Garlate, is Monte Barro, the summit of which is a well-known view-point. I say 'well-known' deliberately: I can do so now, but until the First World War Lecco was seldom visited by travellers from abroad. Perhaps the menace of the Brianza still hung over the Lago di Lecco : the bad reputations of places, like those of people, are not easily erased from the memory. Or perhaps the few writers who did go there, bemused by the beauty of the Como Arm, failed to appreciate the comparative austerity of its landscape. Be that as it may, as a tourist centre it lagged behind its neighbours.

The threat of invasion by an Austrian army soon changed all that. Here was an enemy who, although not so ruthless, was infinitely more to be feared than the robber lords in their eyries. So a military road which is a series of tunnels was hurriedly completed, cutting straight through the flanks of the mountains, which slope sheer down to the water, and linking the town of Lecco with Colico at the other end of the Lake. It is one of those long, fascinating roads (you will find more of them round Garda) along which you drive alternately through tunnels of darkness and bars of light where the balustrades gleam white against the water; and – more important – it is a road along which the columns of Alpini and Bersaglieri could move unimpeded when they were rushed up to hold the Alpine passes. And where the soldiers went, tourism and trade followed.

Quite apart from the ever-present fear of forays from the Brianza, Lecco has a story history. In the fourteenth century it saw much of the fighting between the Visconti and the Torriani – the rival factions whose leaders were contending for the Dukedom of Milan. The town chose the losing side, and was taken and sacked by Azzone Visconti, who later enclosed it within walls and built that magnificent bridge, the Ponte Grande, which spans the out-flow of the Adda river. It has since been 'improved' and much of its character lost, for it now has ten arches. Originally there were eight, with a drawbridge at each end of the bridge.

In the Piazza there stands a statue of Lecco's most famous son – the novelist and dramatist, Alessandro Manzoni, to whom the town owes so much reflected glory. His greatest work, the novel *I Promessi Sposi* ('The Betrothed'), is set in Lecco and the surrounding district during the Spanish occupation of the seventeenth century, and was described by Sir Walter Scott as 'the best ever written'. The novelist lived at the Villa Caleotto, which is now a literary shrine for one of the most revered gods in the Italian pantheon. Other, lesser claims to fame are the open-air market and the annual fair on Easter Monday to which the peasants come flocking from miles around. Like all continental junketings, it is well worth seeing.

And now you are faced with a choice. On the eastern side of the Lecco arm there are one of two places which you may consider worth a visit: Mandello, which is a convenient base for the ascent of Monte Grigna, and Lierna – once a Roman station and famous for its marble quarries. Some of this black Lierna marble was used in the construction of Como Cathedral. You can continue round the Lecco arm as far as Varenna, where the car-ferry will take you back to Bellagio. But my advice is either to return to Bellagio by boat or, if you have your car with you, to take the highroad which runs along the ridge of the Brianza. The scenery is glorious and you will enjoy it – but only if you are an experienced driver with a good head for heights.

After leaving Lecco, then, follow the Erbe road, past the twin lakes of Alserio and Pusiano as far as Erbe, where you turn right and then right again – and so, steadily mounting, to a little place called Asso where, strictly speaking the High Brianza begins. Ahead of you, on your left, is the long crest of Monte Palanzola. Then you climb past Monte Primo, Megreglio, and Civenna with its twin towers which, you will remember, you saw high above you on the way to Lecco. In the clear, almost blue mountain air, it is a wonderful changing panorama as you begin to go downhill until, at one point, a turn of the road reveals all three branches of Lake Como spread out like a map for your guidance. Ahead of you, far away beyond Colico, you can see the silver peaks of the Alps, and presently – down – down below – all the beauty of Bellagio in its triangle of green. For the last few miles the road drops in a series of hairpin bends which have been described as 'vertiginous' – loop after loop, with very little space between you and Eternity – until at last, while your heart is still in your mouth, the lush gardens close in around you, you pass the Villa Serbelloni, and the sound of the traffic and the café orchestras comes wafting up from the town. And then you are in the midst of it – quite a hubbub after the quiet uplands – and there is your hotel with, if you have judged it well, just time for a bath and a change before you sit down to a good dinner and a bottle of Barbaresco.

The Colico Arm

Menaggio, to which you should now cross by steamer on your way to visit the Colico or northern arm of the Lake, may not be a very interesting place but it is important, not only as a commercial centre but because of its position. Here, where the Lake is at its widest at one end of the Centro Lario, the town is situated on a small promontory which lies at the eastern end of the valley which leads to Lake Lugano by road and rail – a short but pleasant journey across a mountainous isthmus.

The opulence and elegance of the villas lining the shore decrease a little as one travels northwards along the west side of Lake Como; but there are picturesque villages, and at Rezzonico, our next stopping-place, there is a tenth-century castle. Rising among cypress trees, this ruin – which is all it is now – once belonged to the powerful family of Rezzonico, which gave to the Roman Catholic Church her Pope Clement XIII. And, going to the other extreme, in earlier days it was the stronghold of lake pirates. It is strange how when people think of piracy – if they think of it at all once their schooldays are over – their thoughts turn automatically to the Caribbean, the Mediterranean, or the Indian Ocean. Some authors of juvenile fiction do not seem to realize that on these Italian Lakes the bad old trade was plied for centuries, if on a smaller scale, by rascals corresponding to the banditti of the mountains, and as dangerous as any sea-rover who made himself feared in Port Royal or Madagascar.

Opposite the cone-shaped Monte Legnone on the other side of the Lake, you will come to the village of Cremia with its olive groves, and its church on the hill, which contains some interesting pictures: a 'Virgin' by Borgonone and a 'St Michael' which is attribued to Veronese. And then, towering above you, you will see the Rocca di Musso, one of the most important castles in the north of Italy and almost impregnable before the days of modern artillery and air power. Ask the people who live in the shadow of Musso if lake piracy is 'kids' stuff'; and if they still remember what happened there, you may receive a dusty answer.

For years this great fortress was held by a man who had made himself one of the most colourful and successful blackguards in the Cinquecento – no mean achievement in a century which saw the downfall of such tyrants as Cesare Borgia and Sigismondo Malatesta. His story is inextricably bound up with that of the lake: Como without Il Medeghino would be like Venice without Casanova. This King of the Lake Pirates (though he would have disowned the title) was an adventurer whose real name was Gian Giacomo de'Medici. He was the brother of Pope Paul IV and the uncle of none other than San Carlo Borromeo. For a reason that I cannot fathom, some writers have tried to turn him into a hero. Brave he undoubtedly was, cunning, and very fortunate. But although he lived to a ripe old age, others – his victims – were not so lucky.

Like some earnest forerunner of Dr Samuel Smiles, he believed in self-help; and, accordingly, began his career at the age of 16 by lying in ambush for another youth, stabbing him very thoroughly, and getting himself exiled from Milan to the shores of Como. In his youthful ambition, he coveted the castle of Musso, which had originally belonged to a small independent republic called the Tre Pievi or Three Parishes and which, he could see, commanded the whole northern reach of the Lake. Il Medeghino's mouth watered for such an eyrie and he played his cards well. By a little lying, a little treachery, and by astutely backing the winning side in the struggle between Milan and the

French and Spanish who occupied Lombardy, he played a bold hand and approached one, Morone, who was Governor of the city. Il Medeghino knew his man and was quite prepared to pay his price, which included the murder of Astorre Visconti who, presumably, was considered dangerous in the city that his family had once ruled. A couple of hired bravos solved that problem, and Morone rewarded him with a letter which, he said, conferred on him the governorship of the castle of Musso.

He underrated Il Medeghino. That young gentleman realized that now the Visconti had been removed, he himself was expendable. Needless to say, he read the letter, and needless to say it contained no word about the governorship of the castle, but ordered the commandant to have the messenger arrested and executed. How Il Medeghino must have smiled at poor Morone's simplicity! History tells us that he altered the letter and thus succeeded in dismissing the garrison of the castle, replacing it at once by men-at-arms of his own choosing.

Securely in possession, he strengthened the fortifications and, by a simple trick and the ingenious use of a double spy, defeated an attacking force with hardly the loss of a man. Then, at exactly the right moment, he changed sides again and deserted Milan for the Emperor Charles v.

The story of Il Medeghino is too long to tell in full, but he became such a legend that he has been awarded a sort of grudging admiration. He levied tribute of course – on the water and in the surrounding valleys; he maintained a small fleet on the Lake – pirates in everything but name; he tried to seize the castle of Arona on Lake Maggiore by treachery; and he even prepared to attack the strong city of Como.

And the end of him? Cannot you guess? He escaped being strung up by the heels, like other criminals of his time; and even persuaded that same Duke of Milan whom he had betrayed to buy his castle and all his lands and ships for the enormous sum of 10,000 gold scudi, plus the title of Marquis of Marignano and a free pardon. He then took service with the Duke of Savoy, fought in the Netherlands and Hungary, and graciously accepted the post of Viceroy of Bohemia. Il Medeghino died peacefully, full of years and honour, in 1555 and in (of all places!) Milan.

We now come to Dongo. With Gravedona and Sórico, it once formed the tiny republic of Tre Pievi which lasted until the Spanish occupation. You will remember that Il Medeghino's castle of Musso once belonged to it. We come, too, to the last chapter in the story of another adventurer, which ended more tragically.

When I first visited Lake Como, people who went to Dongo were taken to see two old churches: the fourteenth-century San Stefano and Santa Maria di Martinico in the hamlet of that name. Santa Maria treasures an unusually beautiful silver cross, wrought in the year 1513 by Francesco Gregorio of Gravedona. But it is our misfortune that times have changed. Nowadays those ancient stones and that exquisite example of the silversmith's craft arouse less interest than the tale of machine-guns on the quay which halted a convoy of German lorries and brought to an end one of the strangest careers in European history.

Accounts of what happened differ; but on a dark, wet night in April 1945, Benito Mussolini, his mistress Claretta Pacetti, and a number of his ministers, made a desperate attempt to escape from Italy before they were overtaken by the Allied advance. They had failed once already; and this time they made their dash for life and liberty in a German motorized column, hoping to escape into Switzerland over one of the passes to the north of Lake Como.

It is probable that most of the planning, however, was done by other people, for it would seem that, by this time Il Duce had lost his nerve. He was within a few miles of safety; but, although he did not realize it, word had reached Italian partisans that the attempt was being made. With their machine-guns on the quay at Dongo, covering the road, they shot up the leading lorry and forced the convoy to halt. There was some parleying; more shots were fired; but Mussolini nearly escaped undetected.

It has been said that, at the last moment, a German soldier tipped the wink to the partisans that the ex-Dictator was in one of the lorries. At any rate, further search was made and eventually he was discovered, cowering in his hiding-place, his grey Fascist uniform covered by a Luftwaffe greatcoat and his helmet pulled down over his eyes. But, as I have said, there are so many different versions of the story that it is almost impossible to find the truth. To quote Mr H. V. Morton: 'Although Drombrowski investigated the death of the Dictator within three years of its occurrence, he encountered so many contradictions and inconsistencies, even on the part of eye-witnesses, that he wrote, "we are driven to query whether there is such a thing as objective historical truth, and to wonder how many lies and distortions lie concealed in the pages of history".'

In this case, all that is certain is that the prisoners were taken to the Courthouse at Dongo, where they faced a summary trial. At the end of it, thirteen ministers were shot out of hand in the Piazza, while their leader and the faithful Claretta, who would not be parted from the man she loved, were taken to the village of Azzano, about 22 miles (35 km) to the south. There Mussolini dined with his captors, and he and Claretta spent their last night together. Then next morning, his mistress still refusing to leave him, they were taken to a near-by lane and 'executed' in cold blood. Mussolini was given five bursts from a sub-machine gun and Claretta Pacetti was shot in the back a moment or two later.

War criminals deserve to die, but what followed was barbaric. As if their death were not enough, the bodies were taken into Milan and hanged by the heels from the girders of a garage in the Piazzale Loreta, where they were exposed to the mockery and ribaldry of a mob which contained (one suspects) many people who, a few years before, would have been shouting 'Duce! Duce!' as they saluted the Man of Destiny. It is good to be able to record, to the honour of the British Army, that one of our armoured cars halted and the officer, with his own webbing belt, secured the skirt of the dead woman above her knees. It was not a popular move. For a minute or two that howling mob showed signs of becoming dangerous. But the officer snapped an order and the guns of the armoured car swung down to calm the fury of the People. There was no further trouble.

The death of Mussolini is ancient history now, but an echo of the tragedy can be heard in a story which is featured from time to time in the Italian Press. It is said that high-ranking officials of the Fascisti came to the Lake at Dongo at about the same time and that there, one dark night, they dumped a lorry-load of bullion. It may well be no more than a yarn for, in spite of intensive searches, the Treasure of Dongo has never been found. But the water of the Lake is deep and – just conceivably – it may still be there, awaiting the more scientific equipment which treasure-seekers of the future should have at their disposal. We shall have to wait and see.

At Gravedona we have almost reached the end of the northern arm of the Lake. It is a pleasant little place, set among trees at the foot of the mountains, but it has played its part in history. In 1178 the men of this town intercepted a convoy and recovered the plunder which the dreaded emperor, Barbarossa, was sending home to Germany by way of Lake Como. These were the days of the famous Gravedona 'Schiffo'. This was a ship on the Lake which, in time of war, served the same purpose as the 'Carroccio' of Milan and other Italian cities. The 'Carroccio' was a high wagon, drawn by oxen, which carried banners, trumpeters, and an altar at which a priest prayed for victory. Like the colours of regiments in later days, it was the rallying-point in battle – the 'soul' of the army, the loss of which meant indelible disgrace.

The castle of Gravedona is a ruin now in the grounds of the Palazzo del Frova, which in 1586 was built for Cardinal Tolomeo Gallio, Count of the Tre Pievi. By this time the little republic was no more, however, and I cannot help wondering why His Eminence retained the title. The fact remains that he built himself a splendid house – a huge Renaissance palace rather than a fortress. But, massive and buttressed, it stands four square on the shore, with a tower at each angle and, on the side facing the water, a handsome loggia. And at the rear of the building there is a little fountain in a dark grove of cypresses.

There are at least two churches in Gravedona which are beloved of antiquaries. One is the Basilica of San Vincenzo. It dates from the Dark Ages but was rebuilt in 1172 and extensively remodelled in the seventeenth and eighteenth centuries. The original crypt remains, however, and is of great interest for, according to some authorities, it goes back to the sixth century. Among the treasures preserved in the church is a beautifully enamelled chalice.

Near by is the little Santa Maria del Tiglio, or St Mary of the Lime Tree, built in the twelfth century on the site of a much earlier church endowed, it is said, by the beautiful Queen Theodolinda, of whom I shall have more to say when we reach Varenna. The present building, which is square, is striped in alternate courses of black and white marble, the deep porch being extended upwards to form an octagonal campanile. On the other three sides are semi-circular apses; and these give the interior, which also possesses a gallery with a barrel-vaulted arcade, an air of great simplicity combined with an austere dignity or even grandeur. This is further enhanced by an enormous Spanish crucifix carved out of a single block of wood – one of those awesome Romanesque, almost Byzantine figures which yet, in some curious way, remind you of certain examples of modern art.

Soon after the end of the First World War, the principal treasures of Santa Maria were stolen and broken up for their precious stones by some ex-soldiers who used a ladder to force their way into the Sacristy – and obligingly left behind them a pocket-book containing two of their names and addresses. We can only hope that they had proved themselves better soldiers than they were burglars, but it is pleasant to record that they had their troubles for nothing. The stones were fakes.

At the end of the Lake there are marshes formed by deposit from the Mera and Adda rivers. You will find villages like

Sorico and Domaso – with the chapel of Madonna di Livo on the hillside above it. And another little place called Gera was the scene of a calamity reminiscent of the Aberfan disaster – though, happily, on a smaller scale. In August 1951 a thunderstorm of unparalleled violence came roaring down from the mountains. In a matter of minutes a small stream had become a raging torrent and fifteen houses with their occupants were engulfed and swept into the Lake by hundreds and thousands of tons of mud and boulders. Fortunately it happened in the afternoon, when most of the peasants were at work in the fields; if it had been at night, many more lives might have been lost. Even as it was, the death-roll was 25.

And so round the head of the Lake to Colico on the eastern shore, where we begin our journey back to Bellagio. Lying among the flat lands and marshes which stretch beyond the estuary of the Adda, this little industrial town is not of great interest to the visitor, but it is important for two reasons. It supplies the whole of Lake Como with its electricity and it commands the military road which leads to the Splügen and Stelvio passes.

A short distance farther south is a curious little land-locked bay – almost a small lake, which is why it is called the Laghetta di Piona; and on the end of the lofty promontory which almost cuts it off from the larger lake, there is an interesting monastery, founded by the Cluniacs in 1138 on the site of a much older foundation. In this, as you may have noticed, it is typical of so many religious buildings in this part of Italy: they are like palimpsests, layer upon layer, till sometimes their foundations, pagan in origin, are lost in the legends of antiquity.

At the turn of the present century the Abbey of Piona was taken over by the Cistercian Order. The cloisters, enriched by columns of granite, marble, and russet brick, are singularly beautiful, while in the little cloister-garth are roses, palms, and exotic plants. Carved on the low stone wall which surrounds the garden, we saw a 'board' for some game of chequers which the old time monks used to play in their hours of recreation.

But their successors, like all good Cistercians, work hard, and Piona is noted for the excellence of its liqueurs. While we were there, a burly brother was selling it in a spacious shop just outside the main buildings.

Kay and I enjoyed our visit to the Abbey. There is an indescribable atmosphere of peace and tranquillity, and also – if I may be allowed the expression when writing of a religious community – of 'good living' in the best sense. Piona is a civilized place. I hope that it is not impertinent of me to say so; but the thought struck me then that, once having brought himself to renounce the world, a man could be very happy there. If you go to Piona you will find simplicity without austerity, no pandering to luxury, but solid comfort. This, of course, is only an impression, but everything we saw (and, naturally, in such a short time we saw very little) was good – of no particular time or fashion but well-made and ageless.

The little church of grey stone, quite plain except for some ancient frescoes, was beautifully decorated with white and salmon-pink gladioli, while the empty Chapter-house, into which I feel we should not have intruded, was finely proportioned; the bare floor of inlaid marble was immaculate, and the stalls for members of the Community were fashioned of some shining dark wood – heavy, plain, and dignified.

We saw a few brothers in their habits of white – or rather, cream – unbleached wool over which, even on that hot afternoon, they wore long brown scapulars. They seemed to be laughing a lot, but they had the quiet eyes of men at peace with God and themselves.

That afternoon we had visited Piona by steamer and, after leaving the Abbey landing-stage, we put back the short distance to Colico, our main port of call. Before us rose the wall of the Alps – slate-grey now and slashed with rifts of shadow and long runnels of snow. A strong wind was blowing in our faces and flecking the deep green of the water with little white horses. For a few minutes languorous Como might have been some lake in the Northland, but for the warmth of the wind, the cypress trees, pink roofs, and walls of ivory and ochre to remind us that this was Old Lario and that we were still in Italy.

On our way home, we passed Piona again and Corenno Plinio which, some say, received its name from Greek exiles with long memories of Corinth. At the top of a flight of steps is the gate of the ruined castle which, in the days of its strength, was second in importance only to Musso. And between the church and the castle there is a small piazza which you may like to see. It contains three fourteenth-century tombs of the Conti Adreani – elaborate, gabled little buildings, carved and crocketed, one of them decorated in that typical Italian fashion of striped marble.

If you are a mountaineer, I have no doubt that you will want to climb the steep cone of Monte Legnone, for which your mouth must have watered when you had your first sight of it across the Lake from Cremia – Cremia with its beautiful belfry down by the shore and its little toy castle perched on the hill. If you are to have your fun it will mean a stay of several days, and I suggest that your best stop would be at Dervio on the broad delta of the Varone. But while you indulge in what I call scrambling about – and what Kay, who loves mountains, calls scaling the heights – I, who do not share your enthusiasm, will carry on to Bellano. It is another of those small manufacturing towns – silk and cotton – and, this time, at the mouth of the Pioverna. Its chief attraction is the deep gorge of that same river, with its two waterfalls; and here you will find all the wild beauty that you could possibly crave without risking your neck on the precipitous crags of Monte Legnone. On several old buildings in Bellano you will see the carved Viper of Milan – evidence that the Visconti once held sway in these parts. And do not miss the fine old church of Santi Lazaro e Celsi with – again – those alternate courses of black and white marble. With a grove of cypress trees rising on the hillside behind it, it would make a perfect setting for some Italianate drama of the Elizabethans.

Travelling southwards from Bellano, the beauty of the surroundings becomes almost breathtaking again, for now you are back in the Centro Lario and when you reach Varenna you can see across the water, the green wooded ridge of the Punta del Bellagio.

The town of Varenna, which marks our next stage, is beautifully situated where the Esino torrent comes hurtling down from Monte Grigna. As I have said, the Lake is at its widest here, and the views are superb. Dominated by a solitary castle tower and by the tall campanile of its parish church, Varenna is set among luxuriant gardens so that, at times, you seem to be walking through the grounds of some elegant villa.

This parish church of San Giorgio is in the heart of the Old Town, which lies just round the bulge of the hill and which many visitors neglect. Built in 1313, it was altered in the seventeenth and eighteenth centuries, and restored to its original state in our own time. It contains some interesting frescoes and a beautiful altar in many shades of marble. A trifle ornate, perhaps, for our taste; but there is also an exquisite confessional of black wood, which caught my eye as soon as we entered the church. It was carved by Giovanni Albiolo of Bellagio in 1690.

The high campanile, which dates from 1653, overshadows the little Piazza of San Giorgio; and here there are two other churches. One is the seventeenth-century Oratory of Madonna delle Grazie, the interior of which is light and simple – baroque, with an altar of black and pink marble and a very handsome reredos, also of marble, black and pink enriched with gold – and again a trifle too lush for those who are used to the little grey churches of England.

The third church carries one back to the Dark Ages, for it is a tiny basilica, very small and ancient – like the aged woman in black whose duty and pleasure it is to explain its beauties. Never in my life have I heard anyone so garrulous: it was like turning on a tap. The whole interior is covered with frescoes in which you can trace the influence of Byzantium; and she led us remorselessly from one to the other, explaining everything in the greatest detail. She never stopped for a moment. I heard Kay make a bid for liberty by murmuring, *Grazie! Grazie!* but she was wasting her breath. The spate of words went on and on – louder and louder, as that little old lady seized on us, as it were, and dragged us, protesting feebly, into every corner of her beloved church. And although our Italian leaves much to be desired, somehow she made us understand. If words failed, she reinforced her voice with gestures; she flung out her arms dramatically; she acted the whole scene. She was smiling and courteous, but as quick as a gnat and – oh, so loud! That tremendous voice of her filled the church. It was strange to hear it issuing from such a frail little body; but she had the spirit and the determination of a fiery young girl. Her eyes blazed with enthusiasm and she made quite sure that we examined that church systematically, inch by inch, before she graciously accepted her *pourboire* and landed us, limp and exhausted, on the Piazza where we reeled into a Bar-Ristorante for a rest and a drink.

When we had recovered a little, we wandered down through the alleys to the Riva Garibaldi, with its brightly coloured houses on the rim of the Lake – red, cream, white and ochre. The lanes are steep and crossed by many archivolts, with here and there on the walls the remains of a fresco or a painted coat-of-arms.

The winding road along the shore and the railway line along which the trains travel to Colico and Lecco, were hewn out of the solid rock, while behind the houses and gardens rise the foothills of the mountains, their lower slopes clothed in woods and vineyards. There you will find deep ravines and pleasant valleys through which you can wander through groves of chestnuts to the village of Esino; not far away are the quarries which yield the black marble of which we have seen so much, and the lumachella or shell-marble; and, within a short walk of the town, is a natural phenomenon which has puzzled many scientists – the Fiume di Latte or Stream of Milk. This comes thundering down through a rocky channel into the Lake; inexplicably, its volume changes – and not only its volume but its

7 *Street of Steps, Bellagio, Lake Como*

HOTEL

colour, for in spring and autumn it looks exactly like a foaming river of milk.

I have spoken of a tower high on the hillside above Varenna. It is said to be all that remains of a castle in which Theodolinda, Queen of the Lombards, spent the last few years of her life. This is not as unlikely as it sounds, although she lived and died among the semi-barbarians of the sixth and seventh centuries, whom one does not usually associate with castles. Buildings – and manners were much more advanced in Italy than in our Seven Saxon Kingdoms. The legacy of Rome lay all around: from end to end of the Peninsula there were fortresses to be copied and, unlike many parts of England, good stone was to be had for the quarrying. Alternatively, the castle may have been enlarged and improved during the Middle Ages, so while it may well be that Theodolinda never saw this particular tower, there is no reason why she should not have lived in an earlier building on the same site.

What is certain is that this beauty from Bavaria, with her blue eyes and yellow hair, was one of those really good women whose deeds the monkish chroniclers could hardly fail to praise. She made roads; she built churches; she gave lavishly to the poor; she performed all those works of mercy and charity which earn an honoured name in history. Queen Theodolinda's kindness and generosity still shine through the ages. But, reading between the lines, what Kay and I find especially endearing about here is that, although she lived in the savage and lurid atmosphere of the Dark Ages, this great lady of unblemished virtue would seem to have been most proficient in what I can only call 'woman-craft'. Blessed with quite exceptional loveliness, she knew every trick and could twist men round her pretty finger with an ease and expertise which one does not usually associate with such saintly characters. She charmed barbarian kings; she charmed her own people; she charmed dry old scribes in the cloisters long after she was dead. Kay even declares that she has charmed *me*.

8 *Limone on Lake Garda*

Theodolinda, who was born about the year 570, was a daughter of the King of Bavaria. She must have had many suitors, but the man who eventually won her was Autaris, King of the Lombards. He wanted to marry her for political reasons – that is, until he saw her: then he just wanted to marry her. But, before that, he had made the first move – an exploit not unlike that of King Erstmere in the ballad. Unwilling to bind himself to a woman whom he had never seen, he made the long journey to the Court of Bavaria in disguise – travelling, it is said, among the entourage of his own ambassadors. Was Theodolinda deceived? The more sedate historians would have us think so, but I doubt it.

The story tells how, when the disguised king reached her father's hall in Bavaria, he and Theodolinda, as etiquette demanded, pledged each other in a cup of wine and that, as they did so, somehow her fingers became entwined with his round the stem of the goblet and caressed his cheek. Again – those old sobersides in the cloisters would have us believe that Autaris was to blame, and again I doubt it. Theodolinda was a king's daughter, even if that king wore wolfskins; and if some ordinary traveller had presumed to take such a liberty, he would have been lucky to escape with a whipping, if he escaped at all. That young woman knew what she was doing. News travels swiftly by word of mouth, as anyone who has lived in a savage country will testify. Somehow she had penetrated his disguise and found him attractive; and, that being so, who can blame her if she gave the poor man a little encouragement?

Whatever the truth of the matter may be, they fell in love – almost at first sight. They were married, and the German princess travelled south with her king into Italy. A charming idyll for those savage days and I only wish that it had a happy ending. But, within the year, Autaris was taken ill and died, leaving his kingdom in the care of his beloved Theodolinda. A woman on the throne! In those days and in any other land it would have meant a protracted struggle for power and bloody civil war. But so devoted were the people of Lombardy to their beautiful queen, so deeply beloved had Theodolinda made herself by her sweetness and grace, that the fierce Lombards begged her to choose whom she pleased for her second husband. They would abide by her decision.

We may be sure that Theodolinda mourned Autaris deeply and long. But for her people's sake and for her own, she had no alternative but to trust herself and her throne to some strong protector. She looked round her half-savage war-leaders and, considering the times she lived in, she chose wisely and well. Her new consort was one, Agilulf, the most famous warrior in her realm – a man who could be relied upon to maintain law and order, as they were understood in those days. He, too, had no chance against her, for she had the audacity to confront him in his own dukedom of Turin; and there, quite plainly and simply, she told him what was in her mind. She did more. No doubt the young chieftain was taken aback: he may even have had some vague idea of weighing the odds and playing for time. But as he bent respectfully to salute his liege lady on the cheek, she gave him her lips, knowing perfectly well that to kiss Theodolinda was to bind oneself to her for ever. Those monkish scribes wrote almost gleefully that she smiled and blushed deeply – adding, I understand, a few improving words about modesty. But I am afraid that they were simple souls and that she was very clever.

From all accounts, Theodolinda and Agilulf were happy and lived together in domestic harmony for 30 years. Side by side, they showed all Italy what enlightened rule could mean, but one suspects that the hand on the tiller was usually the Queen's. When they married, Agilulf was a heathen; but at about the same time that, many miles away – and again at the instance of a woman – St Augustine was baptizing Ethelbert, King of Kent, Theodolinda persuaded her warrior husband to become a Christian.

You may perhaps wonder why I have told the story of Queen Theodolinda at such length; but, if you go to Italy, you will find that after 1,400 years she has not been forgotten. The memory of her presence still haunts the shores of Lake Como – a memory of beauty beyond compare and of goodness which you will find it hard to match in the pages of history. You can still travel the road named after her – the Strada Regina, along which she used to be borne in her litter to bathe in that rich valley of the Upper Adda which is called the Valtellina. And, as you will have observed already, her name is linked with a number of churches and religious institutions.

As a sign of his appreciation of a lifetime spent in doing good, the Pope – St Gregory the Great – sent her many costly gifts. In those days, the capital of the Lombards was Monza, not far from Milan; and there, in the Cathedral, you can see what is called Theodolinda's Treasure. It includes, among personal possessions, her famous 'Hen and Chicks', made of silver-gilt with jewelled eyes and said to represent the seven provinces of Lombardy. And, most precious of all, the collection contains that small golden circlet which is believed to contain one of the nails used at the Crucifixion. I have spoken before of this Iron Crown of Lombardy, with which the Holy Roman Emperors were crowned from 1311 until the days of Napoleon and Ferdinand the First.

From Varenna you can take the car-ferry back to Bellagio.

The Como Arm

Our next objective is the city of Como and there are several ways of reaching it from Bellagio. You can follow the motor-road on either side of the Lake or you can go direct by steamer. They are few and far between but, by careful planning, it can be done. We did it. But, if you can afford it, I suggest that, for a change, you hire a motor-boat to zig-zag from side to side across this south-western arm of the Lake. It is expensive, but it will afford you constantly changing and unexpected views of the scenery and enable you to savour to the full the delights of travelling by water. But perhaps I should have said as near to the full as you can get nowadays if you are not one of those lucky people who make their voyages under sail. There used to be more of them; but, unfortunately, now that the days of the sailing *luciè* are over, men with the time to wait on the wind are becoming as rare as those giant trout which are said to have once lived in the shadow of the High Brianza.

But whether you choose a public or a private craft, by water is the way for, to my mind, one of the minor joys of life is that strange sense of remoteness which only comes to you when you are leaving a town or a village by water. You have just been to the place; you have walked in its streets; you may even have slept there or, at least, dined and talked to its inhabitants. Yet as the ship draws away from the quay, it is as if a magic wand had been waved. Everything becomes unreal. Those little people, growing smaller and smaller as they go about their business, look like walking dolls behind some invisible veil of enchantment. You almost feel that a sheet of glass has been interposed between you and the landing-stage. You have only travelled a few hundred yards from the shore, yet already you are worlds away. And this dream-like yet strangely fascinating experience will be yours not once but many times if you take my advice and go to the city of Como by water.

I think you should begin your journey by crossing to Cadenabbia on the western shore, just opposite Bellagio. Although it is only a hamlet in the parish of Griante, Cadenabbia, together with Lenno and Tremezzo – to the second of which it is linked by a long line of plane trees – forms the Tremezzina district, so renowned for its beauty and for the fertility of its soil, that it has been called the 'Garden of Lombardy'. Griante has been outgrown by its precocious offspring and, indeed, has little left that it can call its own but the picturesque old church of San Martino on the hill. Tremezzo, on the other hand, rising in terraces on the lower slopes of Monte Crocione, and Cadenabbia, where Verdi composed 'La Traviata', have heard and heeded the modern message to keep moving with the times. Really one township nowadays, they have become an ordinary but excellent resort where pleasant, conventional people with pleasant, conventional ideas should find everything they can possibly want to give them a good holiday: luxury hotels, trendy bars positively asking to be propped up, tennis courts, sailing, dancing, swimming – and all these things in a superlative setting with the white houses of Bellagio shimmering across the water. Good luck to them! Their tastes are not mine; but then, as Kay has pointed out reprovingly, it is not everyone who enjoys poking about old churches and castles, or drinking beer in some little *trattoria* among the poor and lowly.

Between Cadenabbia and Tremezzo stands the Villa Carlotta, which is rightly considered to be one of the gems of the Centro Lario. This great mansion was built in the middle of the eighteenth century by the Marchese Giorgio Clerici, a Milanese nobleman who gave it his family name. The house has had several names, real or fictitious, for it appears in Stendhal's novel, *La Chartreuse de Parme,* as the Casa Sommariva, after a later owner. When this Conte Sommariva died, his widow sold it to Princess Charlotte of Prussia, and she gave it as a wedding-present to her daughter, who again renamed it – the Villa Carlotta.

Inside, among many beautiful things, there is a small museum of works by famous sculptors. It includes the relief frieze by Thorwaldsen, 'The Triumphal Entry of Alexander into Babylon', which was commissioned in 1811 by Napoleon to decorate the Throne Room of the Quirinal Palace in Rome. Waterloo put an end to that project and in 1828 the frieze was still in the plaster-cast stage. It was then that one of the Conti Sommariva had it completed in marble; and he is represented, together with the sculptor, at the end of the procession. The collection also contains Canova's 'Repentant Magdalen' and his 'Cupid and Psyche' to which Kay, who had only seen copies, immediately lost her heart; but which so overwhelmed Alphonse Daudet that, as he tells us, he embraced it!

Near the edge of the Lake is a small piazza shaded by palm-trees, and a charming little rotunda chapel, white and cool. It contains a Pietà by Cacciatori and also the vaults of the

Sommariva family, so it was excluded from the sale of the property to Princess Charlotte. But the pride of the Villa Carlotta is, quite understandably, the garden. Behind magnificent wrought-iron gates lies a vast domain of groves, terraces, and formal grounds. Thanks to some magic in the soil – or the loving hands of generations of gardeners – plants grow here to a size and in a profusion seldom seen elsewhere. The tall hedges of azaleas and rhododendrons are quite remarkable; there are camelias and magnolias which will make any gardener envious, formal terraces, pools half-hidden by waxen water-lilies; cedars, cypresses and palms, and wild thickets as dense and green and mysterious as a tropical jungle. Having wandered through the gardens and wished that we had not missed the full riot of colour by coming too late in the season, Kay and I sat on a stone seat in the hot sunshine, watching the lizards on a low wall and listening to bird-song as glorious as any that we have heard in Sussex.

For some years now, the Villa Carlotta has belonged to the Italian Government and, as well as being a great tourist attraction, it is used for conferences and concerts.

At the southern end of the Tremezzina, where the River Acquafredda flows into the Lake, lies Lenno. This is mainly a holiday resort, but for the interested minority there remains the crypt of San Stephano. Here again the authorities differ as to its exact age and I am not expert enough to venture an opinion. I have seen it dated fourth century and I have seen it dated the eleventh: all I can tell you with any certainty is that San Stephano was built on the site of a Roman temple and incorporates remains which are evidence of its pagan origin.

The small tongue of land jutting out into the Lake just south of Lenno was once called the Dosso di Lavido or, alternatively, the Dosso d'Abido. Nowadays it is usually known as the Balbionello Point for when, in 1790, Cardinal Darino built a villa there, His Eminence, in jocular mood, gave it this name as a pleasant diminutive of his other residence, Balbiano.

Originally it was not meant to be a private house but a home of rest for Franciscan friars. It is an elegant building with a particularly fine portico, and stands in a spacious park, while poised on the balustrade at the edge of the Lake and reflected in the water, is a delightful statue of St Francis, holding out his hands in welcome.

The more sombre side of the Cardinal's character must often have been in the ascendant, however, for it is said that his bedroom was hung with black, that he slept in a black four-poster, and that the most prominent object to meet his eyes on waking was a black coffin. Later the property was sold to the Marchese Arconati–Visconti and acquired its present name of the Villa Arconati.

During the struggle for Independence the house received guests very different from the Poor Brothers of Saint Francis – guests who sometimes arrived at dead of night and whose presence was a guarded secret. In 1820, Silvio Pellico, patriot and revolutionary, was arrested at the Villa on suspicion of being a member of the proscribed Carbonari; one of the greatest architects of United Italy, Giuseppe Mazzini, took shelter here from his enemies; and the 'Revolutionary Princess', Christina Trivulzio Belgiojoso, used to be rowed up the Lake from her great grim Villa Pliniana, near Torno, to help the conspirators with her counsel and her active support.

Still travelling southwards along the western shore, we come to the Isola Comacina or Isola San Giovanni, as it is sometimes called – the only island in Lake Como. It is quite small, less than half a mile long and about 400 yards wide; and it is separated from the mainland by a narrow strait, the Zocca dell' Ólio – a name which pays tribute to the richness of the neighbouring olive orchards.

Its fortifications were demolished in the middle of the twelfth century, but once there was a little town on the island which made its mark in history. For 600 years, while the whole of Europe was in the melting-pot, it somehow managed to survive the successive waves of barbarian invaders which came rolling down through the Alpine passes; and, with the exception of Ravenna, it was the last place in the north of Italy which remained loyal to the Byzantine Emperor at Constantinople. And that, I think, is the most remarkable chapter in the history of the Italian Lakes. Just consider what it implies in terms of courage and endurance, of knowing when to bend before irresistible force and when to stand firm, which retaining at all times and against all the odds, some measure of freedom and independence. Six hundred years is a long time and Isola Comacina is a very small island.

It was Theodolinda's first husband, Autaris, who in the end laid siege to the town for six months and forced it to surrender; and it was characteristic of her magnanimity that it was her influence which secured the garrison an honourable capitulation and spared them the sack. Although this war had stolen half her short married life with Autaris, she was the most generous of enemies, befriending the artisans of Como who, as the Magistri Comacini – the Master Builders of the Island, had made this stronghold a city of refuge for the few remaining guardians of the dying Roman culture, and employed them on the Cathedral which she was building at Monza.

In 1169 the town was besieged again and taken by the combined forces of the Tre Pievi and the City of Como; and, this time, it suffered all the horrors of war. It was then that its fortifications were dismantled and it never rose again to power. Its last brief appearance in history was in 1848 when Isola di Comacino became a place of internment for 1,500 Croatian insurgents.

Since then the island has become almost deserted – except on one day of the year. On Midsummer Day (the Feast of St John) a procession of priests, gorgeous in full canonicals, encircles the island in decorated boats. In a cloud of incense, their silken vestments shimmering in the sunshine, they land to celebrate Mass in the little church; and afterwards a fair is held – the Fiera di San Giovanni. Kay and I have not seen this particular festival but we have witnessed similar celebrations on the

Austrian Lakes; and believe me, both the religious processions and the junketings afterwards are well worth seeing.

Here, on the Eve of San Giovanni – at least, until quite recently – great fires were lighted on the mountains which had nothing to do with the Roman Catholic Church or its saints. Such survivals can still be found all over Europe. They are akin to our own Morris Dancers and corn-dollies, and the Beltane Fires of Scotland – relics of cults which were hoary and old and wicked when Christianity was young, and involved worship of the horned god, fertility rites, and certain other ancient practices which are best forgotten.

You should now board the steamer again and cross the Lake to Lezzeno, and here again you will be reminded of wickedness in bygone days. The setting could not be more appropriate for, in contrast to the smiling countryside on the western shore, the landscape is bare and rugged, and Lezzeno itself, lying at the mouth of a gorge, is so steeply overhung by the precipitous spurs of Monte Primo that it is said to be almost without sunshine during the months of winter.

And the story of this village is as grim as its setting. Those fires on the hills and other – worse – things, added to the already evil reputation of the place, brought down upon it, in the sixteenth century, the terrible thunders of the Church. No doubt the real purpose of many denunciations was the settlement of some private vendetta; but the Holy Inquisition was enthroned at Milan and Como, and the Hounds of God were never averse to a witch-hunt. With his hand on the leash and eager to loose them, was that friend of the poor and hammer of heretics, San Carlo Borromeo, whom we have already met in happier circumstances on Lake Maggiore. This stern ascetic, quite confident that he was doing the work of God, let loose all the pains of Hell on the luckless villagers of Lezzeno. There were great slaughterings in the public squares of Milan and Como, and those of his victims were accounted fortunate who escaped with a simple burning. According to documents of the time, San Carlo and others like him urged their executioners to drive out the Devil by inflicting on those poor sinners more and more appalling tortures. And all, of course, with the very best of intentions. All in the name of Christ.

Somehow I do not think that I shall ever like Lezzeno, and even in Milan and Como there is still a faint reek of the faggots. So my advice to you, when you have seen all you want of this tragic place, is to climb up into the clean air and, if you have time, follow a winding path high above the Lake to Nesso. This is another village in a gorge, in which the houses seem to cling desperately to the sides of the ravine. Or if you are one of those people who love mountains, why not climb Monte Primo? You will be rewarded for your trouble by magnificent views of the distant Alps, dominated by Monte Rosa, the highest mountain group in Italy, and, nearer at hand, the long green ridge of the High Brianza.

Nesso is really a commune or small group of villages in the foothills above the Lake, and many people think it worth while to take a small boat up the *orrida* or narrow rift in the rock to see a well-known waterfall. There are the ruins of a castle destroyed by the Sforza in the sixteenth century, a rather forlorn little fortress – just broken walls and three feeble-looking little towers like those of a toy fort. And only two kilometres (about $1\frac{1}{4}$ miles away) is the little church of Santa Maria di Vicu su Nesso, with some faded but interesting frescoes and a diptych of 'The Assumption' by Bartolomeo Benzi.

Then, of course, you could cross the Lake again; but, unless you are prepared to go out of your way, I would advise you to miss Argegno and Moltrasio or visit them some other time: it will be well worth your while. Argegno, where you can take the funicular to the village of Pigra, high in the mountains, is a little market-town, old and picturesque, at the beginning of the Val d'Intelvi, which lies about half-way between Menaggio and Como. Moltrasio, too, has its charms. At the opening of another small valley, its colour-washed houses rise in terraces along the flanks of the hills, and it is a quiet and attractive little holiday resort. Why then did I suggest that you should postpone your visit? Merely because there are so many fascinating villages on the eastern shore; and, as your ultimate objective is the city of Como which will, or should, take up a lot of your time, your best plan is to continue towards the fishing-village of Torno. But first – the Villa Pliniana.

It must, of course, be pure coincidence that this eastern shore of the Como Arm, often so much harsher and more rugged than the smiling beauty which faces you on the other side of the water, should, on the whole, have grimmer tales to tell. It is strange. But it is so. And there is no better example than the story of this famous villa which stands on the shore of a bay, the further arm of which is the little headland where lies Torno.

The great house was built in 1570 in the shadow of a semicircle of dark hanging woods – a vast, gloomy barrack of a place, bleak and pale as a skull against the dark, wooded precipice which guards it from the rear. It rises like some huge mausoleum on the edge of the water, and yet it is so withdrawn into cliff and trees that the sun only penetrates at midsummer. You must not look here for lush gardens, for flowery terraces and roses, for this was the house of a man who was trying to escape from his enemies and from his own conscience. The only sounds are the crash of a waterfall and the intermittent bubbling of a spring behind the courtyard, a spring which rises and falls – no one knows why – and which is mentioned in the letters of the Younger Pliny, who owned a country house on this site and after whom the villa was named. Yet Napoleon Bonaparte chose to stay here after the Battle of Marengo; and Shelley was so entranced by the weird, almost sinister atmosphere of the place that he expressed a desire to rent it for a season. A house for ghosts, if ever there was one; but for its story we must plunge into the darkest depths of the Renaissance.

In the sixteenth century, nepotism was rife in the Vatican as elsewhere, and His Holiness Pope Paul III did well for his natural children. The worst of them, Pier Luigi Farnese, had been created Duke of Parma and Piacenza, and even in the blood-stained annals of his time he had few rivals for sheer wickedness. In 1540 he was responsible for a ghastly massacre at Perugia and he was guilty of an unspeakable outrage on the Bishop of Fano about which even the history books are reticent. There were numerous other little peccadillos and it is inconceivable that this cruel tyrant should not have known that he was playing with fire. Perhaps he thought that, as the Pope's bastard, he was safe from retribution. If so, he was mistaken. There was the inevitable conspiracy. In the palace at Piacenza, some of his nobles, headed by Count Giovanni Anguisola, surrounded him suddenly, stabbed him, cut his throat, and threw his carcase out of the window in the time-honoured fashion. They can be regarded as assassins or public benefactors – whichever you please. But, after some years as Governor of Como, the murder began to prey on the mind of Giovanni Anguisola and he built this villa as a refuge from the Papal avengers. But there was no escape from his own thoughts, which cannot have been very pleasant. And that is just one reason why I would not care to live at the Villa Pliniana. As Kipling would have said, the Feng-shui or spirit of the house may be evil.

One who apparently did not think so was Princess Cristina Trivulzio Belgiojoso, 'the Joan of Arc of Italy', whom I mentioned when I was telling you about the Villa Arconati. In the stirring days of the Risorgimento, this most admirable lady occupied the house. She, too, could have been called a conspirator – but how different from that tragic assassin! Beautiful, accomplished, charming, courageous, she spent several years of exile in Paris, fighting with her pen in the cause of Italian liberation. Then, in 1848, she joined the Piedmontese in the field, having raised a regiment of volunteers which she commanded in person. After a succession of reverses she was again banished from Italy, but later she helped Garibaldi to defend Rome against the French. And in the intervals of her stormy career, her home was the Villa Pliniana. A great lady and a great patriot. Perhaps I was wrong about the Feng-shui.

You have yet another villa to visit on your way to Como, but before you cross the Lake to Cernóbbio, you will be wise to spend some time in the romantic old village of Torno. You will have to go there by boat, however, for traffic cannot enter. There is no road, only a flight of steps which leads down past the church into the little piazza.

Like so many of these Lake villages, Torno was built on a point of land jutting out into the water. It has been described as looking 'comparatively uninteresting' when seen from a boat, but with this verdict Kay and I cannot agree. With its campanile, its picturesque harbour, and its garden walls washed by the water, it seemed to us everything that an Italian fishing-village should be. An ideal sanctuary for anyone who longs for peace and quiet. There is something very soothing in the thought that cars are excluded.

Colourful houses and gardens line the shore with, here and there, a little inlet running up between the walls, while beyond the harbour, as I have said, is the miniature piazza from which steps lead up into the outer world. The whole village is a series of alleys mounting the hillside, and there are two churches. The parish church of San Giovanni has a fourteenth-century doorway and treasures, as its most precious possession, a nail which is believed to have been used at the Crucifixion. The other church, Santa Tecla, has a Lombardic façade and, like San Giovanni, a portal of the fourteenth century – in this case, surmounted by a rose window. And even the cemetery or Campo Santo of Torno is laid out in rising terraces. Between the funereal cypresses there are fine views across the Lake.

Torno, with its little harbour, where you can sit in the shade and watch the boats and the glittering water, is an attractive haven to those who, like us, are content with simple things. Yet even this idyllic spot has known what it is to sup on horror. During that long-drawn agony which we call the Italian Wars of the sixteenth century, when hireling armies from half the countries of Europe made the Peninsula their stamping-ground, Lodovico Sforza, Duke of Milan, called in French troops to bring his turbulent subjects to heel. There was a French garrison at Torno – though where all those men were quartered is anybody's guess. But, like most mercenaries, those men-at-arms were not averse to making a little money 'on the side' and presently Sforza woke up to the fact that they were filching too much of his trade. So, very foolishly, he brought in the Spaniards to redress the balance – and got more than he had bargained for. Torno was sacked by the Spanish soldiery and appalling atrocities were committed. Nowadays – and quite understandably – we think we know all about the horrors of war. So it might be as well if, just now and then, we had a good look at the campaigns of those picturesque ruffians with their huge plumes and slashed, particoloured clothes – *landsknechte* and others, fantastically dressed like a pack of monstrous court-cards. A long, close, steady look. Then perhaps we might change our minds.

And now we really must cross to the western shore and Cernóbbio, only five kilometres (just over three miles) from Como. It is an elegant watering-place, gay with colourful villas and gardens; it possesses a good beach and an excellent small harbour. But there is little else to detain you for, when Cernóbbio is mentioned, most people think at once of the Villa d'Este, which lies just north of the town.

The Villa d'Este is now an hotel – one of the finest and most luxurious in the world. It is also very expensive. So I need hardly say that it is beyond the means of a freelance writer. But many years ago, before I was married, I once trailed round those stately apartments with an escorted party of tourists – an experience that I would not care to repeat. For once, too, it was a grey day with, if I remember rightly, a slight drizzle. So that huge park and the gardens with their looming statuary were not looking their best and those vast saloons could hardly have been described as 'cosy'. He would have been a bold man who dared to smoke a pipe there.

Yet I must be fair. My first impression of the famous villa was demonstrably false. Unlike the ocean in the American song, it really is 'all that it's cracked up to be'. For the very rich it is the answer to a problem, for there they can find everything they want – or nearly everything. There can be no doubt that the Villa d'Este gives value for money: princely rooms which contain many beautiful works of art, a superb cuisine, complete efficiency, and a service most deft and self-effacing. At least, that is what I have been told and I am quite sure that it is true. There is a Country or Sporting Club open all the year round, an 18-hole golf course near at hand, tennis courts, a lido, and every kind of water sport; while in May and June, at Cernóbbio, there is show-jumping for the Concorso Ippico, which attracts some of the finest riders in Italy – indeed, in the world.

The Villa d'Este has been the residence of sovereigns and princes of the Church. Built in 1568 by Cardinal Tolomeo Gallio, it was once the property of Princess Amelia Elizabeth of Brunswick. Then, in the nineteenth century, it was purchased by Count Perro, who later became a political exile in the cause of Italian freedom. In his time, a frequent if clandestine visitor was Princess Cristina Trivulzio Belgiojoso, who used to go there for secret meetings of the patriots.

Before her time, however, the great house gave shelter to a very different and far less admirable lady, for the Villa d'Este was the Italian residence of Caroline of Brunswick, wife of our own George IV. Hard things have been said about 'Prinny' and he was certainly no saint; but, from all accounts, the behaviour of his consort would have shocked even our permissive society. I will not sully what a Victorian would have called 'this pure page' with an account of her most undignified amours; but here at the Villa her equerry and courier, Colonel Bartolomeo Bergami, was in constant attendance and, according to reliable authorities, there were 'goings on'. This was nothing new for, both as Princess of Wales and Queen, Caroline had made herself a centre for scandal. For years she had gone just a little too far, even for Regency England. By the time she was uncrowned Queen she had become a joke, and there is little doubt that she

9 *Sirmione on Lake Garda*

HOTEL DU LAC

deserved the squib which, at the time of her trial in Westminster Hall, ran round the country like wildfire:

> *Most gracious queen, we thee implore*
> *To go away and sin no more;*
> *Or if that effort be too great,*
> *To go away at any rate.*

The City of Como

Como – episcopal see of Lombardy and the largest city in the province and on the lake which bears its name, is in direct communication by road and rail with Milan and, by the St Gotthard route through Switzerland to the rest of Europe. It is a great manufacturing town and centre of the silk industry which flourishes on the white mulberries which grow on the Plain of Lombardy – although nowadays, of course, a large proportion of the silk is artificial. It is also a place of exceptional interest to the art lover and the historian and, surrounded as it is by beautiful scenery, it is an excellent base for holiday-makers, whatever their tastes may be. Como can be all things to all men. Here you can sail or swim or dance, spend your time happily examining historical monuments – or merely laze with a drink in the sunshine, beside some delightful companion, talking quietly or just watching blue-green water flecked by flickering silver wavelets.

The city began as a lake village built on piles during the Stone Age, but since those days it has known many masters. Celt, Roman, Byzantine, Goth, Hun, Lombard, Spaniard, and Austrian: each in his turn has been Lord of Lario. In Roman times Como was a military station with the usual forum, baths, gymnasium and theatre, and traces of its occupation by the legionaries still remain. Then, when Rome had fallen and the sky was darkening, Belisarius came from Constantinople to salvage what he could from the wreckage and reunite the lost province with the Eastern Empire. He was followed by Narses

10 Gardone on Lake Garda

– old and a eunuch, but one of the greatest statesmen and generals that the Dark Ages produced. The situation was almost hopeless but he helped the Lombard rulers, including Queen Theodolinda, who owed a loose allegiance to the Emperor, to maintain some sort of law and order, and sow the seeds of a new Christian culture.

In the twelfth century there was desperate fighting between Como and Milan, with sieges, assaults, and great battles of armed galleys on the Lake. It was not until 1335 that Como was ceded to the Visconti; and even then his rule must have been loose, for in 1450 his successor, Francesco Sforza, found himself obliged to besiege the city and carry it by storm. It was another Sforza, Lodovico – he who was called Il Moro, because of his dark complexion – who introduced the silkworm into Lombardy, an event more important than all the feats of arms in the history of his house.

In the Middle Ages, like so many other Italian city-states, Como was rent by feuds and street fights between the adherents of two great families – in this case, the rival clans of Rusca and Vitani – until, in 1439, the rivals were solemnly reconciled by Fra' Bernardino of Siena. We should remember such things when we read of the Church's intolerance. But the Renaissance, for all its blessings, brought the darkest period in Como's history – 159 years of Spanish rule, which lasted until 1714. The unhappy city was dominated by the priests who, in their turn were watched and controlled by the Holy Inquisition. Young people were forced into convents or into the service of Spain, and the Piazza del Duomo saw all the fantastic horrors of the 'auto-da-fé', when men and women became burnt offerings for daring to worship God in their own way. In 1603 the population had dwindled to 6,000 souls.

In course of time the Spanish overlords gave place to the Austrians; the land became less priest-ridden, and the torture and bloodshed lessened. But there was still oppression; and when the Risorgimento brought hope of freedom, the Comasci were not the people to submit tamely to alien rule.

In 1859 the Battle of San Fermo was fought over the mountain passes just south of the city. The Austrian general, Marshal Urban, though he outnumbered Garibaldi by two to one, made the fatal mistake, when facing an enemy on the heights, of weakening his striking power by leaving a large force in Como, where it was able to take no part in the fighting until it was too late. The Garibaldini, charging with the bayonet, carried all before them with their superb *élan* while their great leader, sabre in hand, was in the thick of the fighting as usual. It is doubtful whether a commander is justified in thus exposing himself. But Garibaldi knew his men. Where he led, they would follow. Soon the plain below was dotted with the white coats of the retreating Austrians; and as the Lake steamers, filled with cheering rebels, paddled southwards to help their countrymen, Garibaldi occupied the city of Como virtually unopposed. Bells clanged in the campanili, bands played patriotic tunes, and excited crowds, cheering and waving, gathered in the streets as he and his tired but victorious *cacciatori* came marching in through the Porta della Torre, near where his statue now stands. With eight battalions of infantry, a battery of guns, and some squadrons of Uhlans, Marshal Urban had no choice but to fall back on Milan. And as he abandoned the city of Como, Liberty marched in. The tri-coloured banner was flying and all the drums beat a welcome.

Como is a wonderful place and I envy you your first sight of it. And if you have been there before, you are still very fortunate, though – I must be frank – nowadays, the traffic is appalling. Screeching motor-bikes, scooters, all sorts of cars apparently driven by fiends, help you to understand the meaning of the expression 'living dangerously'. In Como and most of the lakeside towns, crossing the road is an adventure. Many Italians are selfish motorists and seem to think that zebra crossings are there to be ignored. Those whom we encountered had no sense of lane discipline, but they had an inordinate love of hooting and of 'hotted up' engines. Week-ends must be a foretaste of Hell – though in fairness it should be added that if you have an accident in Italy and have not sounded your horn, you are in trouble.

Even in the alleys you are not safe, for small boys on bicycles do their best to imitate their misguided elders. One urchin, whizzing round a blind corner in one of the back streets of Como, collided with me violently, came off, and lay in the road, howling dismally. A slightly older boy, probably his brother, saw what he thought had happened and pedalled away at top speed, yelling 'Giovanotti! Giovanotti!' at the top of his voice. Kay and I had visions of being stoned by all the young ruffians in the quarter.

I do not blame that boy: I admire him. All he had seen was Little Brother lying on the ground, screaming, and a large foreigner with a heavy stick standing over the innocent victim. Yet when he failed to rally his 'Giovanotti' he came back alone to face the brute. Fortunately, Little Brother was more frightened than hurt; Kay has a way with small boys in tears; the small crowd which had collected dispersed; there were smiles all round, and everything ended happily. But it could have been very unpleasant.

The crown of the city of Como is its great marble cathedral. John Addington Symonds, who knew and wrote so much about the country and its architecture, declared the Duomo to be 'perhaps the most beautiful building in Italy for illustrating the fusion of the Gothic and Renaissance styles'.

The present building, dating from the fifteenth century, arose on the site of an eleventh-century basilica, the architects being Pietro da Breggia, Florio di Bontà, and Tomaso Rodari – the 'Maestri Comacini'. The west front is pure Gothic with a magnificent rose window and three doorways with rounded arches, decorated and carved. On either side of the central door are figures popularly supposed to represent the Elder Pliny, who died heroically, trying to save people during the Vesuvius eruption which destroyed Pompeii, and his nephew who has come down to us as the Younger Pliny. Both owned villas on the

Lake and both – as was customary in the Middle Ages – are represented in medieval costume. Anyone in Como will tell you that they are the Plinys and who am I to contradict them? But why they should have been commemorated in this way remains a mystery.

Another mystery is a hideous frog carved among the stone foliage which adorns the jamb of the north doorway, sometimes called after it, the Porta della Rana. And thereby hangs a tale. I will tell you the story later on, but first I would draw your attention to another feature of the building. I refer to the delightful little pinnacles and crockets which rise on either side of the roof and which are most elaborately and exquisitely wrought. I admit that the idea may be fantastic, but I have always thought that they resemble miniature church towers by Sir Christopher Wren. An architect would smile, but that is what they look like to me.

The interior is the very antithesis of any of our old English cathedrals, being built of the black marble of Olcio and the white marble of Musso. As to architectural style, the nave is pure Lombard Gothic and the chancel High Renaissance. The 10 bays of the aisled nave soar up to a groined roof, and there are some good reliefs and carving by Tomaso and Filippo Rodari, especially in the south aisle, where there are six representations of 'The Passion' by Tomaso Rodari (1482) and, near the south door, the altar of Sant' Abbondio, rich with carving and gilded woodwork. Here, too, there are pictures: 'The Adoration of the Magi' by Luini, and 'The Flight into Egypt' – considered to be one of Ferrari's masterpieces.

Not far away is another of his paintings, 'The Marriage of the Virgin', Luini's 'Virgin and Child' and, farther east 'The Descent from the Cross' by the Rodari. These late medieval artists were nothing if not versatile – architects, sculptors, painter, carvers; and here in the Duomo you can see another of Tomaso's reliefs, 'The Virgin and Child with St Louis and St Stephen'. You will find it in the north aisle between the busts of Bishop Ravelli and Pope Innocent XI.

In the chancel, below the magnificent High Altar, is the golden throne of the Bishop of Como; but, to us, the one unforgettable experience in this vast cathedral was to stand beneath the central dome and look steadily upwards. There is nothing to impede your sight. It soars and soars up and up until you almost feel that if it were any higher it would soar into infinity. This mighty masterpiece is not so old as the rest of the Cathedral, having been added by Juvarra in the eighteenth century.

In the Piazza del Duomo and adjoining the Cathedral, is the Broletto or City Hall, built in courses of black, white, and pink marble. On the other side of it is the Communal Tower, grey, solid, and four-square. It was originally erected in the thirteenth century; 200 years later, the upper storey was added; and then – although you would never guess – it was rebuilt in exactly the same form in 1920. To me, the Cathedral, Broletto and tower are the most evocative group of buildings that I have seen in Italy. Some years ago, in Venice, Kay and I were lucky enough to witness part of a pageant of the Middle Ages and Renaissance, for once beautifully and correctly dressed. It was a wonderful experience. The surcoats and houppelandes and armour – rich, sombre colour and dull steel against the shimmering water of the Basin of St Mark – carried you back through the ages as surely as if you had walked into a painting by Gentile Bellini. Yet, somehow, I think that those men and women would have looked even more at home if they had paraded before the striped façade of the Broletto at Como. To me, that range of buildings: cathedral, city hall and tower, breathes the very spirit of medieval Italy – a strange, turbulent world of merchants and men-at-arms, of civic pomp and civic violence. It is the perfect stage, waiting only for the actors and actresses.

Another building which you should see in Como is the basilican church of Sant' Abbondio, named after the patron saint of the city. It is simple to the point of austerity, but it is very old. The present building goes back to the eleventh century, but a pattern of black slabs inlaid in the paving marks the outline of the original church, which was built 600 years earlier, and outside the east end may be seen pillars which once supported the fifth-century narthex or vestibule.

In the oldest part of the city, near the Cathedral, there are narrow alleys and handsome stone houses with painted shutters, and, here and there, cool courtyards like Spanish patios. There are fine modern shops in Como, smart hotels and restaurants, which could be anywhere in Italy. But in the side streets there are little cafés and wineshops where, among more respectable beverages, you can buy that crude spirit called *grappa*, akin to the Yugoslav *slivovitz* for both of which, to Kay's intense disgust, I must confess a fondness. There is also an early nineteenth-century theatre – something even dearer to my heart.

This old Teatro Sociale behind the Cathedral is built on the site of a small castle which was called the Round Tower and held by the Rusca family until it was occupied successively by the Visconti and the Sforza, lords of Milan. The harbour of Como was once defended by a towered rampart. It has long disappeared, but the city retains an impressive section of its walls. The Porta della Torre, through which Garibaldi entered in triumph, is surmounted by a twelfth-century tower – hence the name, though in commemoration of the patriots' victory in 1859, it is also known as the Porta Vittoria. There are two other gateways remaining – to the east and south-west of it respectively – the Torre di San Vitale and the Torre di Porta Nuova; but all that is left of the Romans' Praetorian Gate is now in the cellars of the Technical College.

When you were on your way to Como, you may have noticed a solitary tower on a hill about a mile from the city. With part of the curtain walls, it is all that remains of the Castello Baradello; and, although there is no longer much to be seen, that ruin has a history. Dominating the village of Camerlata, the castle was occupied by the German Emperor Barbarossa, on the night before his overwhelming defeat by the Milanese at Legnano. And, in 1277, Napoleone della Torre and several members of his family were exposed in iron cages on the wall by Ottone

Visconti, Archbishop of Milan. It is said that Napoleone went mad and dashed out his brains against the bars of his cage. So much for the Days of Chivalry! The stronghold was finally dismantled in the sixteenth century by the Emperor Charles v.

And now for the story of that Frog. I have saved it, so as to end on a less sombre note and because it is rather a rarity. History has bequeathed us many records of suffering and slaughter, but tales of medieval practical jokes are few and far between.

As I have hinted, the famous Frog is one of the sights of Como Cathedral, but I had better say at once that this annoying little reptile is very difficult to find. We knew where to look – just outside the church, on the jamb of the north doorway. But where exactly was it? There are, of course, two jambs and both of them are covered with the most elaborate and intricate carving. After searching the maze of sculpture unsuccessfully for a long time, we appealed to a priest who was about to enter the Cathedral – a rather austere-looking young priest who unfortunately knew no English. In those days neither Kay nor I knew the Italian for 'frog' and we were not helped by the fact that, for once, we had no dictionary with us. I tried acting the part; but my performance, faintly reminiscent of 'Toad of Toad Hall', only brought a steely glitter into those chilly eyes and the priest drew himself sternly erect, firmly convinced that I was mocking him. It was only when one of us remembered that last resort of the traveller – drawing, that our amateurish little sketch produced a smile of understanding and quite a genial young priest pointed to that elusive Frog among the carving. As frogs go, it is not up to much, but the story may interest you.

It began in the year 1850, when a priest from the village of Introgna, not far from Locarno, announced that he possessed an ancient document which said that a treasure was to be found beneath the Frog on the north doorway of the Cathedral at Como – that ugly stone reptile about which several legends had already grown. Where he found the document I do not know; but, at the request of the Como authorities, he produced it; it was examined by experts, and declared to be genuine – a piece of writing dating from the late fifteenth century.

Briefly, the message of the manuscript was as follows. He who dug beneath the Frog to a depth of eight *braccia* (about 16 feet or 5 m) would find – first, an iron chest full of silver; beneath that, if he went on digging, another chest containing a corpse; and, beneath that again, a third chest full of gold.

The priest and others whom he had interested in the quest asked permission to excavate; and, after the usual delays and procrastination, permission was eventually granted by the City Fathers – who, in those days were, presumably, the Austrian authorities.

The work was not begun until the May of 1852, but then it became a nine-days' wonder, eagerly watched – and, no doubt, impeded – by the Comasci of all classes. And what happened? Nothing. It was a complete fiasco, for all that was found beneath the Frog was a spring of clear water.

The disappointed crowd turned ugly. The embarrassed treasure-seekers were met by hoots, jeers, catcalls, and rude gestures, though their frank opinion of the unfortunate priest has not been recorded. Yet – and this is the point – everything points to the fact that the manuscript was genuine. Some of the greatest experts in Italy had examined it with care: ink, parchment, handwriting. So what are we to believe? As I have said, I am sure that the only possible solution of the mystery is the obvious one. Some medieval humorist perpetrated a practical joke, the consummation of which he could never hope to witness. Or could he? Were the experts all wrong after all? Was that parchment a modern fabrication? I have never heard it said before, but surely the answer lies in the history of the document *before* it came into the hands of the priest. Or something quite unexpected may have happened in the fifteenth century. Perhaps the parchment was lost. It may only have been by accident that the jester's little joke was forgotten for 400 years. We shall never know. Sometimes I wonder whether that wicked old Frog does!

3. Lake Garda

The Western Shore

Garda, the southern end of which lies midway between Brescia and Verona, is the largest lake in northern Italy, being over 31 miles (50 km) long and from two to 11 miles wide ($3\frac{3}{4}$ to $6\frac{1}{2}$ km). Isolated as it is from the other great lakes, from England it is reached by flying to Milan or to the Villafranca Airport at Verona, while by road or rail, the way from the north runs over the Brenner Pass. There is also a bus service from the Piazza Castello at Milan.

This great sheet of water, in places more like an inland sea than a lake, is divided between the provinces of Verona, Brescia and Trento. It is fed by the Sarca river, which enters in the north at Torbole, and is drained by the Mincio which flows out of it at Peschiera on its way to join the Po.

The Romans had never heard of Garda : to them it was always Lake Benacus, and even in the Middle Ages writers never seem to have been able to make up their minds what to call it. Dante used both names. But all through history it has been renowned for its beauty and notorious for its storms.

Compared with the Tre Lagi, its conformation is simple. There are no arms and its shape is rather like that of a slightly curved tobacco pipe with its bowl towards the south. This southern end is wide and surrounded by flat country gradually rising to low hills, its shore dotted with villages, villas and vineyards, while the northern basin – the stem of the pipe – is long and narrow, with steep sides, like a Norwegian fjord. Here, too, there are villages and villas – where they can find a foothold, but the water is bordered by mountains which become higher and wilder as you travel northwards, for not far away are the Dolomites and a region of beetling crags, pines and cataracts, which until the First World War formed part of the Austrian Tyrol. This part of Italy is a place of contrasts. On a journey which took Kay and me deep into the mountains to the north of Lake Garda, we passed in a few hours from a soft southern scene of cypresses, vineyards and palms, of pink-tiled white houses, and churches with slender Italian campanili, to sharp Alpine air, wooden chalets, the German tongue, and – we were lucky! – the sight of an eagle.

At the southern end and jutting out into the Lake, is a tree-covered tongue of flat land, 2½ miles long and in some places only 130 yards (118 metres) wide. This is the peninsula of Sirmione and it is here that we will begin our journey, travelling up the western side of the Lake and back again down the eastern shore. There is a motor-road right round the Lake and the steamer service is excellent.

Near the end of the promontory you should cross a bridge to the little town which clusters round the thirteenth-century castle built by the Scaligeri family when they were lords of Verona. It is a most formidable fortress surrounded by a moat and immensely thick walls with high, crenellated towers. With its fish-tail Italian battlements, it looks rather like a fairy-tale castle, almost too good to be true; but it is real enough and, by commanding the bays of Peschiera and Desenzano, to east and west of the peninsula, it dominates the entire southern end of the Lake. Dante was a visitor here, and in 1276 the Bishop of Verona and the Inquisitor of Mantua held another of those ghastly burnings of heretics at Sirmione, 100 of them being immolated that orthodoxy might be preserved.

There is a small piazza and there are narrow arched streets, while in the fifteenth-century church of Santa Maria Maggiore you can see ancient colonnades, the pillars of which proclaim that you are again on the site of a heathen temple. In Roman times, Sirmione was a refuge for wealthy patricians who, lost to the world in this remote peninsula of olives, fig-trees, and oleanders, could idle away the hours very pleasantly in the gardens of their villas, sample the water from the warm sulphur springs, and pledge each other in Lugana wine from the vineyards near Peschiera. No intense heat and no mosquitoes. Just blue water, white marble, and willows. There is little that we could have taught rich Romans about the art of living.

The most famous of those early visitors was Gaius Valerius Catullus – the greatest lyric poet that Rome produced, and the sworn enemy of Julius Caesar. The latter answered the most scurrilous attacks by entertaining Catullus lavishly – a gracious vengeance which showed the world the measure of his greatness.

In a grove of trees on the extreme tip of the peninsula are ruins which some say were public baths in the days of the Emperor Constantine, and others – hopefully – the Grotto of Catullus. If, indeed, it is the remains of a Roman villa, it is the largest in northern Italy; and many maintain that it was here, in his beloved Sirmio, that the poet mourned his false Lesbia. Gazing at the grey ruins in the olive grove, one thinks of the new hall for congresses, the open-air theatre, and the water-skiing school. All very good. But what will be left of them in 2,000 years' time?

Travelling westwards along the short southern shore of the Lake, you will come to Desenzano. Here on the plain are groves of fruit trees – olives, oranges and lemons, and one understands why Lombardy is famous for rice, cereals and flax. Looking away to the North, where Lake Garda narrows so dramatically, you can see the mountains closing in, knowing that, far away, the horizon is the jagged line of the Alps.

Desenzano is an important tourist centre on the Milan–Venice railway. There are excellent connections by road and water to all parts of the Lake, and two harbours – the small inner one, surrounded by arcades and weeping willows, being the more picturesque. Mounting guard over the town is a tenth-century castle, built on the site of a Roman fort, the original purpose of which was to repel invaders from what is now Hungary; and in the church of Santa Maria Maddalena, you will find some good pictures, including a 'Last Supper' by Tiepolo. But if you are not in the mood for uplift and are temporarily bored by the restaurants and lidi provided for your delectation – well, you could do worse than simply amble about under the arcades, watch the boats and their reflections dimpling in the water, and drink the excellent local wine in some little bar or café. Unless, of course, it is Tuesday.

Every Tuesday morning there is a market in Desenzano, and I think you know my partiality for continental markets. This one grew out of the Roman granaries of Decentia and for centuries was the principal market for grain in northern Italy. Under Venetian rule, magistrates took it in turn to sit in the building called for some reason La Patria, to stamp bills and contracts, and to see that the market laws were obeyed. Like most of the laws of the Serene Republic, they were wise but rigorous, and are exemplified by the rule which decreed that no outsider could buy grain until the local needs had been satisfied.

Within easy reach of the town are two villages with names which became famous during the War of Independence. Each has its tower. The Torre di San Martino commemorates Victor Emanuel's victory over the centre and left of the Austrian army on 24 June 1859, while on that same bloody Midsummer Day, Napoleon III crushed their right wing at Solferino. There, an old Scaligeri tower looks down on what is surely one of the most important battlefields in modern history, for it was there that the Swiss, Henri Dunant, while on holiday, was so appalled by the hideous aftermath of the fighting on this and other fields that he wrote his 'Souvenir de Solferino'. It was this unvarnished account of the suffering endured by the wounded of both armies, published in Geneva in 1862, which led to the Geneva Convention and the institution of the International Red Cross. The flag of Switzerland has never won more glory than when, its colours reversed, it is carried on to some battlefield to help lessen the misery and pain.

To the west of Desenzano lies Padenghe with its castle and more Roman remains; and it is here that we turn north along the western shore of the Lake. At Moniga there is a seventeenth-century villa once occupied by the historian, Pompeo Molmenti, and beyond that we come to the villages of Manerba and San Felice. It is a broken shore, very beautiful, with cliffs and bays and inlets. Farther on still, there is a bold promontory and the Isola di Garda – an island with a history. In the ninth century the Emperor Charlemagne presented it to the monks of the monastery of San Zeno in Verona, as a place of retreat for quiet meditation; but it was 400 years later that it became known as the Friars' Island, for St Francis of Assisi bought some land there and established a small community of Minori Oservanti.

The friars flourished. They, too, were visited by Dante (doubtless when he was a guest at Sirmione) and we are told that he delighted in theological disputes with the brethren. Later, the fiery St Bernadino of Siena, the 'people's preacher' who reconciled the feuding factions in Como, encouraged the Franciscans to enlarge their house, which eventually became a well-known theological school. It was suppressed in the eighteenth century.

Thereafter the atmosphere changed and Isola di Garda became involved in the struggle for liberation. In 1817, the island, its buildings neglected and half in ruins, its gardens overgrown, was purchased by Count Luigi Lechi, who replanned, rebuilt, and transformed a jungle into a thing of beauty. A peaceful paradise – on the surface; but all through the first half of the nineteenth century, Isola di Garda was a headquarters of the patriotic societies who were waging ceaseless underground war against their Austrian overlords.

As you will have realized already, this so-called Romantic Age was the heyday of the secret society in its most theatrical form: cloaked conspirators, midnight meetings, countersigns, dark lanterns and daggers. All the appurtenances of old-fashioned melodrama were there, for that was the Italian way. But it should never be forgotten that behind what we prosaic northerners would call the histrionics were brave men ready to fight and die for freedom, or to drag out the years in the soul-destroying darkness of a dungeon. There were times when men such as these charged with the bayonet in battle and won – simply because they could only be issued with 10 rounds of ammunition. And it was the same when they confronted the enemy alone. They would shout a slogan or strike an heroic attitude even when facing a firing-squad; so although we may smile at their theatricality, we can only salute their courage. All through the years of the Risorgimento the struggle against the oppressor went on – but not at Isola di Garda, for one day, during Count Luigi's absence, there was an unexpected raid. A printing-press and compromising documents were found by the police and the island's use by the patriots had come to an end.

And so to Salò, where gradually the ground begins to rise. The long stretch from Salò to Gargnano is what is loosely referred to as the Gardone Riviera, which claims to be one of the loveliest lake districts in the world – a claim often made in Northern Italy and always with good reason. The sheltered Brescia Shore of the Lake is warmer than the Verona side and rich with luxuriant vegetation: cedars, cypresses, vineyards, oranges, lemons, and fig trees in profusion, grey orchards of gnarled and twisted olives on the lower slopes of the hills, and – anywhere they can find root-hold – aloes, wild capers, and sweet-scented mints. The Riviera, as its name suggests, is a civilized district of well-kept villas, lakeside hotels, bathing lidi and esplanades. There are formal Italian gardens with balustrades, voluptuous statuary, and flower-beds like emblazoned banners laid out in the sunshine – gardens which seem to be waiting for love affairs or dark intrigues under the cypresses. Places for cigarettes rather than a pipe, for sauntering and sipping wine, rather than striding manfully up the mountains which are now so invitingly near at hand.

Old Salò (the Roman Salodium) with its walls and towers built by Beatrice della Scala, no longer exists. Most of it was destroyed in the earthquake of 1901 – including the bell-tower built to resemble the famous Campanile at Venice, which itself collapsed from sheer old age only a year later. Luckily the Cathedral with its triple nave, polygonal apse, and massive pillars was spared, so the religious processions for which Salò was famous continue – including the Good Friday Procession of which it has been said that 5,000 candles are on the move. And in one of the chapels is a crucifix which Mantegna declared was the most beautiful in Italy. In Salò, too, you will find a street called the Via de' Violini, for those famous musicians, the brothers Bartolotti, were born in the town, and one of their sons, Gasparo of Salò, invented the violin as we know it today.

But this sunlit stage has been darkened for tragedy; and, as on Isola di Garda, it was full-blooded melodrama, for in one of the suburbs of Salò stands the Martinengo Palace, and this great house was the scene of our own John Webster's play, *The White Devil.* Built by the Venetian Commander, the Marchese Sforza Pallavicino, in 1585, it was the refuge of two fugitives – the villainous Duke of Bracciano and the beautiful Vittoria Accoromboni, notorious for her 'innocent-resembling boldness' and already found guilty of adultery and murder. The Duke, too, had murdered his first wife and Vittoria's late husband. Not an unusual situation for those days but, unfortunately for Vittoria, her husband had been a nephew of the powerful Cardinal Peretti and, still more unfortunately, the Cardinal had assumed the Papal Tiara as Sixtus v. The White Devil had nearly run her course. On the sudden death of the Duke (and in Conquecento Italy sudden deaths always gave rise to suspicion) and the discovery that his first wife's family had been disinherited, she realized that she had been caught up in a ruthless vendetta. In this emergency she recalled Pallavicino's friendship and decided to seek the protection of the Venetian

11 Roads cut from the cliff Riva, Lake Garda

Republic. She escaped from the Martinengo Palace but her enemies were at her heels and at Padua they caught up with her. How shall I put it? She died.

The Martinengo family, of whom it is said that 'the history of Brescia for a thousand years could not have been written without reference to them', have left their mark on Salò. In the next century Count Camillo Martinengo-Cesaresco, a man with the sensibility of an artist and the morals of a robber-baron, displayed to the world the strange dual nature of his kind by terrorizing the neighbourhood while he lived and bequeathing to his heirs when he died one of the most beautiful gardens in the whole of Italy. But there was one condition and it was typical of the man. Determined to be a despot even in death, he made it obligatory in his last will and testament for every future inheritor of the Palazzo Martinengo to assume the name of Camillo and thus perpetuate his memory. Could vanity go further?

For a short time during the Second World War, Salò was the seat of the Fascist Government.

Beyond the Gulf of Salò we come to the town of Gardone, which gives its name to the Riviera, though a few stalwarts – local patriots – maintain that this lovely stretch of shore should really be called the Salò Riviera. Gardone is a pleasant holiday centre situated where the Lake narrows and the mountains begin. From now on, the Gardesana Occidentale, Mussolini's splendid motor-road along the western shore of the Lake (below the older Penale Road) runs through a series of 70 or 80 curving tunnels on its way to Riva. In summer the whole of the highway is ablaze with oleanders. As you drive along you pass through alternate areas of deep shadow and gorgeous sheets of colour set against the intense blue of the water.

The Cathedral contains some interesting pictures, but Gardone's chief attraction is that of a modern and luxurious resort where you can enjoy all the sports on land and water which appeal to the average visitor. Yet the town has its title

12 *Near Malcesine on Lake Garda*

to fame as the retreat and the last resting-place of one of the most flamboyant yet courageous leaders that even Italy has produced, for near Gardone is the Vittoriale – that great complex of buildings to which Gabriele d'Annunzio retired after his abortive attempt to annexe Fiume at the end of the First World War. If ever there was a man born out of his time it was d'Annunzio. In an earlier century, as a condottiere, he might have carved out a dukedom. He had already made a name for himself with his sensuous and colourful verse when, from the crucible of war, the erstwhile decadent emerged as a hero and patriot. Like von Richthofen, he turned from the cavalry to the air: he lost the sight of one eye, but his exploits against the Austrians were fantastic. Then, as if this were not enough, he fired a small army with his eloquence and held the port of Fiume for 15 months, defying all the politicians of Europe. Of course he failed. The odds were too heavy. He was forced to realize at last that the days for such adventures were over, and sheathed his sword in the Vittoriale, where he died in 1938.

On either side of the next promontory lie Toscolano and Maderno. The former was once the principal Roman settlement on the Lake and the place where some forgotten landslide may well have given rise to the legend of the lost city of Benacus, sunk beneath the waters of the lake which once bore its name; while the latter is the only town in the district which perpetuates the memory of Venetian rule by a column crowned with the Winged Lion of St Mark. Other places worth visiting in this built-up area of the Riviera are Fasano, Bogliaco, and Gargnano. A certain amount of industry is carried on in Gargnano, but it is chiefly of interest to the stranger for the church of San Francesco, its Franciscan friary, and its delightful waterfront – a line of villas and gardens, bowered in trees, on the very edge of the Lake. Then come Bogliaco, Tignale, and Tremosine – this last perched on a plateau over 1,000 feet above the water. Tremosine is also accessible by a narrow and dangerous road through the gorges of the Val Brasa. The views are breathtaking but the route is not recommended to those who are unused to mountain motoring. Seen from the Lake, Tremosine looks almost as if it were hanging in space.

You are now more than half-way up those narrows which have been likened to a fjord – deep in the long funnel where the mountains sweep sheer down into the water. A few little hamlets or groups of houses hang on where they can; and there is one spot called the Hungry Meadow which can only be supplied by boat – and then only when the Sover or the Gra are not blowing. The Sover is the great wind which comes roaring down from Riva at the head of the Lake and the icy peaks of the Dolomites only a few miles to the north. Confined by the bottle-shaped conformation of the Lake itself, the force of it – and its opposite number which blows from the south – churns the water into angry waves flecked with white spume and causes those sudden storms which make Garda the roughest of the lakes. They do not happen very often or last very long. But when the Sover blows, the fishermen put in to the nearest shelter, and the husbandmen pray for their orchards and vineyards on the tiered terraces. It is against these winds that the terraces are covered with the white pillars of pergolas, glazed or latticed to give some protection against the storm. But when the sun shines on this, the bluest of all the lakes of northern Italy, the rows of white pillars in ordered ranks lend such beauty to the scene that one is apt to forget their grim purpose.

They are to be seen at their best at Limone, the most northerly of the resorts on the western shore. The village clings to the rock in a sheltered position, flanked by enormous cliffs. A fertile spot, in which every inch of ground is built on or cultivated, and its inhabitants are justly proud of the fact that it grew the first lemons in Europe. Hence the name. Above the huddling houses are the tiers of terraces, but one is always conscious of the loom of the mountains which look as if they were ready to sweep this lakeside village into the water to share the fate of Benacus.

Kay and I arrived at Limone on the steamer, landing on

the tiny quay near which, at one of the little cafés, they brew what must surely be the worst tea in the world. The British Army used to be famous for the strength of its 'char', though none that I ever tasted equalled that devil's brew at Limone. But let us be fair. Its flavour was amply redeemed by the smiling courtesy with which it was served.

There is not much to see at Limone, but I am told that the hotel accommodation is good, and it has that air of peace and tranquility which is above all price. There is an old church with some good pictures and an 'onion' spire to remind you that Austria was once very near. For the rest, it is a place beloved by photographers and artists – a fascinating jumble of old houses which look as if they were tumbling over each other down the hillside, cobbled streets and narrow alleys where one walks in single file, now deep in shadow, now ablaze with sunshine. And there are a number of dark, mysterious shops which tempt you to explore. Kay and I would like to return to Limone one day – but not at tea-time.

Looking at Lake Garda as it is today, with its peaceful inhabitants and carefree visitors, its hotels and villas and sailing-clubs, it is difficult to realize that there was a time when it became necessary to build a castle to afford some protection against those perennial pests, the lake pirates. The site chosen was at Riva (the Roman Ripa) at the northern end of the Lake.

Riva – or, to give it its full name, Riva del Gardo – is by far the largest and most important town on the Lake. It has become a popular and prosperous holiday centre and a mecca for tourists from all over Europe. The impression that remains with me is of sunlight, sparkling blue water, and a colourful crowd – as colourful, surely, as anything seen in the Middle Ages. Under gay striped awnings and café umbrellas I rejoiced in the sight of brawny, sun-baked ladies in backless dresses and Mexican sombreros, and their sweating escorts in shorts and tee-shirts, with cameras slung round their necks, and funny little straw hombergs – like Joseph's coat, of many colours. Trippers?

Certainly. British – American – Italian – Germanic – of all sorts and sizes. But then, who *is* a tripper but somebody else on holiday? Have you ever thought of yourself as a tripper? No, I thought not. Neither have I.

Feeling pleasantly smug and superior then, you had better light a cigarette or one of those long, thin Italian cigars, and set about seeing such things in Riva as are worthy of your notice. I think you will find quite a lot of them – and lots of other people too, who prefer not to proclaim that they are on holiday quite so blatantly. The Austrians fortified these hills which guarded the gates of Tyrol; and nowadays, in an air-lift, you can ascend to the Bastion in five minutes, sit on the terrace and enjoy a really remarkable view of the northern end of the Lake, with the pink roofs of Riva far below and, away on the left, the incredible castle of the Counts of Arco, perched high on its precipice like something out of a Walt Disney film.

In Riva itself, down by the waterfront, is the Piazza Tre Novembre, where you will find medieval arches, palaces and porticos, and, dominating the town, the fourteenth-century clock tower called the Torre Aponale – sturdy and plain. On the other hand, if you have a taste for the Baroque, you might care to visit the somewhat ornate Inviolata church, on the road to Arco: many good judges find its elaborate interior very beautiful. And near the Piazza is the Rocca – that moated stronghold built in 1124 against the pirate raids. It is a museum now, with many interesting exhibits, not the least of which is the building itself, with its fine courtyard and machicolated gateway. But so much to be seen there is fascinating. Kay had to drag me away from the ranks of faded photographs of those men of Riva who fought in the wars of the Risorgimento. There they are, those white-bearded veterans who, such a very few years ago, used to hobble slowly down to their favourite tavern to drink with their old comrades – a slowly diminishing band, as old comrades always are. But in these pictures they are still young, still active, still soldiers, with bristling black moustaches and eagle eyes. I am aware that it is a truism but it struck me that morning with renewed force. There is something awesome about the camera and something very sad.

And it is from Riva that you can take, if you will, a short spell away from the great lakes. For a few hours or a few days you can experience a complete change of atmosphere in the scented pinewoods and sharp tonic air of the Brenta Dolomites. When we were there it was early June, but the spring flowers were still out in the high places and I especially remember the beauty of the deep blue gentians. The mountains themselves are more majestic than any travel brochure has dared to suggest; and, if you have no taste for winter sports, there is much to be seen during the summer months. But you must be prepared to forget sophistication and find content in simple pleasures: the kiss of the cold spray from the waterfalls, the wreaths of mist veiling and unveiling the high peaks, and the shafts of pale sunlight slanting between the tall pillars of the pines. You will be rewarded with marvellous views across the snow-clad teeth and pinnacles of red Dolomite rock; you can visit the little lake of Ledro and many smaller mountain tarns, and cascades like the famous double-falls of Valesinnella, where you can drink beer at the little inn and watch a sight that you will never forget. Then, if you have to return, as we did, after quite a short visit to the mountains, or if you are lucky enough to penetrate deeply into what, until 1918, was part of the Austrian Tyrol, you will come back refreshed to appreciate more and more the warm, sensuous beauty of the southern culture. It is all so different up here on the Border, so much wilder and more primitive. I have already told you how we saw an eagle circling among the crags, with its huge size and slow, flapping wings, it was unmistakable. I cannot imagine that bird anywhere near the Gardone Riviera. A few venturesome chamois may still live in the mountains which border Lake Garda; but here in the Dolomites, at a little inn where we stopped for a drink, we were shown the photograph of an elderly but amiable bear who makes an occasional public appearance. It is all very sad. Thanks to the march of Progress, he has learned to scrounge.

And on that journey, as so seldom happens, the best part was reserved until the end. The drive home. For once there was no anti-climax and the run back to Riva was quite an experience. As far as I can remember, the wooded Pass of Bardino, which drops down from the bare uplands, is not quite so dangerous as the descent from the Black Mountains of Montenegro. But our driver was taking no chances. There were the usual hairpin bends, the same appalling precipices and overhanging cliffs, the same sudden glimpses of the road far, far below. With only a few inches between us and eternity, we crawled.

Near the village of Campo we passed a lonely monastery of Capuchin monks; and now the solitary chalets with roofs of grey pine-slats were becoming fewer, their place being taken by typical Italian cottages and farms. There is a castle at Campo; but presently, by the beautiful green lake of Tandau, we saw the first of the real robbers' nests – a ruined stronghold on a crag, as menacing as anything to be seen in Germany. Then we passed another – and another – till one of us remarked that paying toll on the Bardino must have been almost as expensive as the passage of the Rhine.

We were now following the course of the little River Sarca on its way down from the mountains to Torbole and the Lake. And so, at last, we came to Riva and the tunnels of the Gardesana Orientale which here, where the Verona shore of Garda begins, cuts through the flank of Monte Brione. The time had come to take the long road back to Sirmione and the south. But there is a lot to see and, if possible, you should do so at your leisure.

The Eastern Shore

Torbole used to be a fishing village but in recent years it has expanded into a small town. The principal industry now is tourism and a very pleasant place it is in which to spend a holiday. Kay and I were there some years ago – long before we ever thought of writing a book on the subject; and although it is in the north, we found that – thanks to the steamer service – it is a good centre from which to visit other parts of the Lake. The excellent hotel which C.I.T. recommended was once the villa of an Austrian nobleman. Rows of prints lining the stairs – pictures of units of the old Imperial Army: Cavalry, Artillery, Infantry of the Line, Feld-Jäger battalions, and so on, were further evidence of how times have changed in this town where the older people are bi-lingual but the younger generation speak Italian.

At this hotel there were, of course, the usual comfortable bar and lounges; but on several occasions, after dinner, I preferred to leave the other guests and stroll round to the other side of the little harbour and under an old arch on which a plaque commemorates the first visit to Italy of the poet Goethe. There, in the more picturesque but unfashionable part of the town, I used to visit a humble *bottega* which I had found, where I could smoke a quiet pipe and drink a glass or two of my favourite *grappa* which has a kick like a mule. There, too, I was able to watch and listen to all sorts of interesting people. I am as patriotic as the next man, but when I am abroad I tend to avoid my fellow-countrymen with their Scotch and bridge and golf. For a short time – although I am sure that it would soon bore me – I like to seek the company of people who have what is to me a strange background; and, from my observation and a word here and there, try to piece together something about them.

Nearly every night there was somebody about whom I might have woven a story, but I suppose the oddest that I met that year were two unpleasant characters in a car, who stopped Kay and me one afternoon while we were taking a walk along one of the less frequented roads near Torbole. They told us in quite good English that they were 'running' watches from Switzerland across several frontiers into Yugoslavia, and were kind enough to offer us one of their watches 'very cheap'. When we politely declined to take advantage of their generosity, they shrugged as only an Italian can shrug, and drove away; and for a long time Kay and I wondered why they had been so foolish as to furnish two strangers with their description and the number of their car – both of which, no doubt, would have been of interest to the police. But then I remembered a passage in one of Charles Dickens's books about a Kentish watering-place in Early Victorian times. It seems that long after smuggling in England had been brought under control, visitors were often accosted by blue-jerseyed 'fishermen' who would whisper that they had a bottle of 'run' brandy for sale – brandy which the visitor could have bought for half the price in the High Street. What they were really trying to sell was not brandy but romance. They knew that all the world loves a smuggler: that ever since the days of Adam, forbidden fruit has been the sweetest.

We have pleasant memories of Torbole, of that quietly elegant hotel and of breakfast under the big magnolia tree in the garden. As I have said, on the other side of the harbour there are steps and alleys and old houses, and the little town possesses the oldest church on Lake Garda. Yet even this peaceful place has echoed to the sound of battle. When the First World War became a certainty, the Italian Alpini manhandled their guns to the heights of Monte Baldo, and so were ready for the attack by their opposite numbers, the Austrian Jägers. But 500 years before, Torbole had found its niche in history, for it saw the end of a really remarkable feat of military transport.

> In the depths of winter, when the passes were closed, Gattamelata, perhaps the greatest of the Venetian condottieri, made a famous forced march across the mountains to the north of Lake Garda; and when, in 1439, it became necessary for the Venetians to send supplies to the beleagured city of Brescia, he ordered one of his subordinates (some say that it was Colleoni; others that it was a Candian engineer named Sorbolo) to transport a small fleet overland from Verona to the shores of Garda, a roundabout journey of about 60 miles.
>
> There were two full-sized galleys and three smaller ones, together with a number of other craft, some of which were

carried on carts. But to move the whole flotilla over the mountains took hundreds of men three months and was a notable feat of engineering requiring the utmost resolution and powers of endurance. The ships were taken up the River Adige, past Rivoli and Moni, and then manhandled over rough mountain tracks to the little lake of Loppio. A great number of trees had to be cut down to provide log-rollers and the rafts on which the keels of the vessels rested, while the motive power was provided by teams of oxen and by teams of men hauling on cables. Slowly, yard by yard, they dragged the galleys up the pass, while other men toiled and sweated, shifting the logs to provide a constant succession of rollers. Lake Loppio gave them a short respite, then that terrible, heart-breaking haul began all over again as the ships were heaved up the mountainside to the village of Nago, high above Garda.

And then the descent began, down a watercourse where a rough path now runs between olive orchards. The descent is steep and the men had to strain at the ropes to prevent the ships getting out of hand and crashing down into the valley. It is probable that this was the hardest part of the whole operation, but it was accomplished at last and the flotilla was launched on Lake Garda at Torbole near Riva.

At Nago, in what is now the Strada Santa Lucia, a stone tablet commemorates this tremendous feat, while in the castle of Malcesine, on the shore of the Lake, there are diagrams and models which show the passage of the ships from Verona to Torbole. There are pictures of the galleys on their rafts, moving over the log-rollers, the teams of oxen, the drivers with their long whips, and the gangs toiling at the ropes as they manhandled the big ships up and down the mountain slopes. (From my history of the Venetian Republic, *The Lion of St Mark,* Bobbs-Merrill.)

Malcesine, which lies about 10 miles (16 kilometres) south of Torbole, is a charming old town, crowded during the tourist season. It is dominated by yet another castle of the Scaligeri; and, as the steamer approaches, the tall, thin maschio tower rears up in front of you like an admonishing finger – the maschio tower being the last refuge of the besieged garrison – the strong place, characteristic of Italian castles. In this case, it rises out of a pentagonal keep, now the Lake Museum, which contains those models and diagrams illustrating the transportation of the galleys across the mountains. It is well worth a visit. There is also one of those horrible oubliettes or dungeons into which prisoners were lowered through a hole in the pavement. The castle, begun in the eleventh century, challenged from its rocky promontory any advance of an enemy from the Dolomites into what used to be the territory of the Serene Republic of Venice.

Between the fortress on its knoll and the long limestone ridge of Monte Baldo lie the old fishing port and orchards of gnarled and twisted olive trees. Malcesine is quite a small town; but you can see the Palazzo Comunale, which was once the residence of the Venetian official known as the Captain of the Lake. It has an impressive façade with pillars and arcaded windows, and in one of the rooms a large fresco depicts the coats-of-arms of the officers who once lorded it there.

As is so often the case in these little lakeside towns, you can profitably spend some time just wandering about the steep and picturesque streets; and, in the course of your stroll, you may well come across the following memorial tablet:

HINC
J. W. GOETHE
ARCEM DELINEAVAT

It recalls how, on 13 September 1786, Johann Wolfgang Goethe, on his first visit to Italy, sat down in all innocence to sketch the castle of Malcesine standing four-square on its little rocky peninsula. But he had reckoned without officialdom. He was seen. He was reported to the Captain of the Lake. And there, in all solemnity, he was informed that he had incurred grave suspicion of being an Austrian spy. With equal solemnity he declared that he was a citizen of the Republic of Frankfurt and, with some difficulty, he was able to prove his bonafides. He was released, no doubt with much bowing and hand-shaking all round, and departed to write a humorous account of the incident in his *Italian Tour.*

The next place to visit on the eastern shore is Torri del Benaco, another fishing-village which has blossomed most successfully into a flourishing resort. The old name of Castrum Torrium tells us that it was fortified by the Romans, but it possesses – need I say it? – yet another Scaligeri castle. This one was built in 1388 by Antonio della Scala, the son of that Cansignorio II whose tomb you will see in Verona. They were great castle builders, the Scaligeri; but life in medieval Italy was, to say the least of it, uncertain, and they were wise to take no chances. In any case, their day was almost over for, after a short occupation by the Visconti of Milan, Verona submitted to the firm but benevolent rule of the Venetian Republic.

Torri del Benaco is another of those places which it is best to approach by water. As you steam southwards from Malcesine you pass a series of islets: Olivo, Sogno, and Trimolene with its forts. The long jagged ridge of the mountain is with you all the way to Monte Maggiore, the highest peak of the range, towering above the water to over 6,500 feet (2,000 metres). But if, instead of stopping at Torri del Benaco, you decide to go on to the town of Garda, you will double the headland of San Vigilio – the most picturesque promontory on the Lake, with the cinquecento Villa Guarienti Brenzone and its little chapel of San Vigilio – pale against the black cypresses. As you round this unforgettable peninsula, where the trees and the walls of the lovely old villa are mirrored in the water, you have reached the place – almost opposite Salò – where the mountains sweep down to the lowlands, the Lake widens, and the great southern basin begins.

The town of Garda, which gave the Lake its present name, has lost all its former grandeur. Of the fortified Rocca little remains except some ruins on a flat-topped hill like a colossal Norman 'motte', which rises above what nowadays is little more than a big walled village. But in the tenth century, under the Carlovingian kings, it was designated a city and there was a time when it was the centre of eighteen dependent communes. Down by the little harbour there is another residence of the Captain of the Lake; there are narrow lanes which the centuries have not changed; and one can only hope that the atmosphere will not be destroyed and that Garda will escape the fate of many historic towns in Italy and other countries, including our own. It would be little short of a crime if this old place was raped by the get-rich-quick boys who, in their greed and craze for trendiness, are only too ready to kill the goose that lays the golden eggs. Like the other old towns on the Lakes, it is too good to be destroyed or disfigured by some syndicate of so-called 'developers' on the make.

As for the Rocca – ruined though it is now, those battered old stones have been a barrier between life and death. In the twelfth century the stronghold stood a year's siege by that most formidable warrior, the Emperor Frederick Barbarossa. And nearly 300 years before that, a drama was played out in the Rocco which would furnish a theme for an historical novel.

First, let us try to visualize the setting. Again – as when you were at Theodolinda's castle on Lake Como – you must not picture some splendid medieval fortalice, for this was the time when the northern races were just emerging from savagery. So the early Rocca di Garda would have possessed no lofty maschio tower, no crenelated battlements or machicolated gateway. There would just have been rough stone walls, very thick and solid – perhaps even earthern ramparts in places, strengthened by a palisade. And the people who thronged the hall and other buildings inside the perimeter would have been just what one imagines in those dawn years of our civilization: shaggy warriors in bright primary colours with, here and there under a wolfskin cloak, the glint of mail or scale armour; their uncouth women

– none too clean, and a swarm of half-naked brats, slaves and hounds. You must think of them shouting at each other, singing and brawling round the winter fire; you must hear horns blowing in the mist, and the sound of storms lashing the Lake as the great wind came roaring down from the Alps. It does not sound very inspiring and certainly not in the least romantic. Yet that shambles was the scene of a very knightly deed, done years before anyone had thought of the beautiful concept of Chivalry.

It was over a 100 years before William the Conqueror cast lustful eyes on Saxon England. In the year 960, Queen Adelaide, widow of Lothar, the Frankish king of Italy, was sought in marriage by the ruthless Berengar of Ivrea – some say for his son: some say for himself. The lady refused him but Berengar was not the man to stop at trifles. He had her seized and carried secretly to his Rocca of Garda, where escape seemed impossible and where he was confident that he could persuade her to change her mind. But he had reckoned without a certain priest who has come down to us as Fra Martino and whose destiny it was to play the knight-errant in advance of his time. We do not know how this brave man came to hear of the Queen's captivity or how he gained admittance to Berengar's lair. Indeed, it seems likely that when the unwilling bride was brought in, he was there already, as chaplain to that brutal crew – God help him. In those early days they had peculiar notions of Christianity.

What is certain is that this kindly priest took pity on the lady, somehow contrived her escape, and, after facing many hazards on a long and perilous journey, delivered her safely to the strong castle of Canossa in Emilia, where she was under the protection of Otto the First of Germany. This emperor – known later as Otto the Great – espoused the cause of Queen Adelaide, defeated Berengar in battle, and – just to round off the story neatly – married her himself. And what of Fra Martino – the man who had risked everything to make it possible? Nobody knows. The great adventure of his life over, he simply faded out of history.

The last place of importance to visit on the shores of Garda is Peschiera – at the southern end of the Lake and separated from the Punta di San Vigilio by the curve of a great bay. But first you should most certainly see Bardolino and Lazise. They may be small, but they rank as resorts and are full of interest and beauty. And, if it is possible, you should go by car, for the road to Bardolino is lined by venerable cypress trees, like dark colonnades through which you can see the gleam of the Lake on one side and, on the other, flat fields and orchards bounded by low hills on the horizon.

Bardolino, built on the site of a prehistoric lake village, is in the heart of the vineyard country: indeed, as every wine-list proclaims, a famous vintage is called by its name. The whole commune is rich with the vine, with fruit, and, above all, with the olives which have earned this fertile countryside the honourable designation of Riviera degli Olivi. There are three ancient churches and, down by the harbour, a ruined tower bowered in trees; but Bardolino moves with the times and those visitors who do the same will find all kinds of sports laid on for their pleasure.

Near Lazise the Autostrada del Sole joins the main motor-way over the Brenner Pass, up which Mussolini marched with his legions when his future ally, Adolf Hitler, showed signs of becoming troublesome. Lazise is a pleasant, leafy little town which still has its walls and a Scaligeri castle from which, in time of danger, an immense chain could be stretched across the mouth of the harbour. In the ancient church of San Nicolo there are the remains of frescoes; there is an interesting old Customs House – a relic of Venetian rule – and a promenade where you can walk among palm-trees or take your ease under the striped umbrellas at one of the little cafés. Is there anything more enjoyable in the gold of an Italian summer than a leisurely glass of wine or beer taken at an iron table that is hot to the touch and from which you can see brightly painted boats and water flecked with sparkling wavelets?

And so, at last, to Peschiera, within sight of the Sirmione Peninsula where you began your journey. It is a famous tourist centre now, on the railway from Milan to Venice, but it has been a place of importance since the days of Imperial Rome. There used to be a medieval castle and a walled harbour: the former was demolished and rebuilt by the Austrians, who needed a fortress where the River Mincio flows out of the Lake. With its town walls and strong military works, Peschiera formed one corner of the famous 'quadrilateral' – those four strong points which commanded the roads into Lombardy.

During the wars of the Risorgimento – in 1848 and 1866 – the Italians suffered two defeats at Custozza, which lies among the hills to the south. But those battles pale into insignificance beside another event which took place over a 1,000 years before, for it was here – somewhere in the green fields which border the Mincio, that there occurred one of the most momentous meetings in history. Europe was saved from an appalling disaster, and life as we know it today was made possible by the faith and courage of one man.

In 452, Attila the Hun – Khan of the Hi-ung-nu – the Scourge of God – who had been defeated the year before by an army of Romans and Goths at the Battle of Châlons, was withdrawing sullenly across Western Europe, leaving a long trail of ruin and desolation behind him. Glutted with blood and plunder, the Tartar hordes from Central Asia had devastated the north-west of Italy and were on the march for Rome – if 'march' is the right word with which to describe that awful surge of thousands upon thousands of flat-faced, slit-eyed savages in filthy sheepskin caps, crouching over their shaggy little ponies and driving before them their flocks and herds, and such prisoners as they had reserved for slavery or a slow death.

Their women and children rode with them, for they were nomads without a home, so it was their custom to encamp for rest and to gorge themelves on their favourite diet of meat and fermented mares'-milk. When, like a swarm of locusts, they descended upon Peschiera, the whole countryside was black with their 'yurts' or circular tents of thick felt; but it was clear that this was only a temporary respite. How could it be otherwise?

13 Lake Orta from Sacro Monte

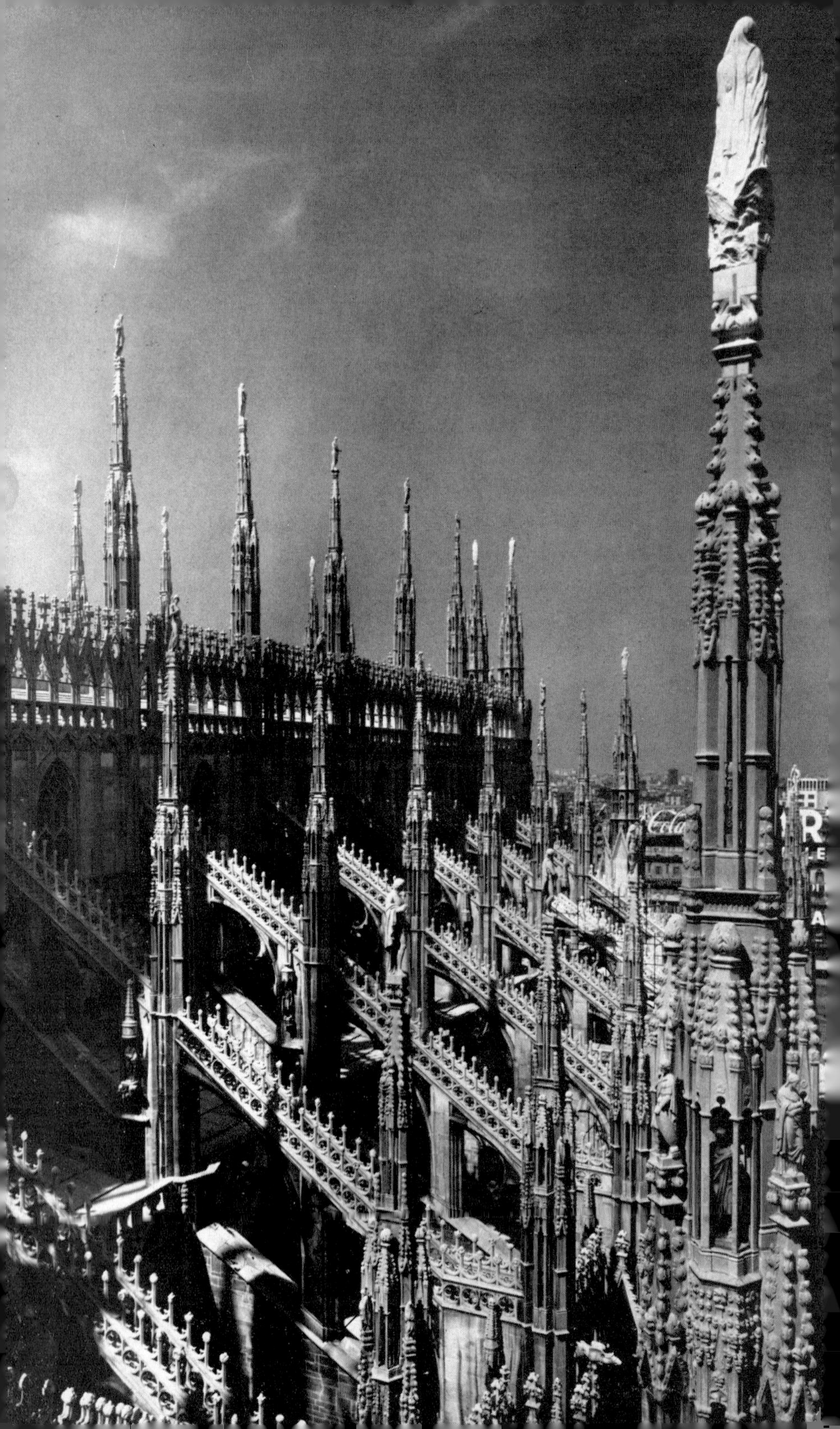

It seemed that nothing could save the Imperial City for, in her decadence, Rome was as supine as an old, sick animal, and neither the Emperor nor his generals were willing to take the field again. That one last effort at Châlons had exhausted the once-mighty Empire. But while the legions held back, the Church prevailed. The hour produced the man.

One day the Tartar sentinels sighted a small body of horsemen advancing towards them – not soldiers but priests and peaceful citizens with, at their head, the Pope himself, Leo I, Bishop of Rome. He was later to be called Leo the Great and canonized as Saint Leo.

This great hero must have realized what would happen to him if he failed. Martyrdom in some unpleasant form – and his bloody scalp decorating the Khan's bridle. But he advanced boldly, almost alone, and confronted that monster from the desert and the steppes face to face. He pleaded. He argued. And – almost incredibly – he won. Attila turned away from Rome and, after laying waste the country as far as the shores of the Adriatic, withdrew with his hordes into the wilds of Pannonia, beyond the Danube. How did Pope Leo do it? Threats? What could he threaten? Bribery? What bribe could possibly have outweighed the sack of Rome? Then what remains? Was it, perhaps, a miracle? We can only wonder. All that is certain is that it happened and that it happened near here – perhaps where you have just parked your car, at the southern end of Lake Garda.

In the Land of the Three Lakes, Maggiore, Como and Lugano are near neighbours. Garda lies apart. Nearly 50 miles (80 kilometres) separate the Western Gardesana from Lecco, the nearest point on Como and, before so many people took their cars abroad, this – the largest of the Lakes, was somewhat neglected by foreign visitors. Now, however, distance is no longer a problem; and, for comfort and convenience, it can hold its own with any rival. Communications, accommodation, sports facilities, leave nothing to be desired and there are times when I am

14 The roof of Milan Cathedral

not sure whether Garda, in its beauty, is not the most rewarding of all. I like the contrast between the mountainous north and the fertility of the southern basin, between the ultra-civilized, built-up areas around Gardone and Salò and the rugged peaks – range upon range – which bound the horizon at Riva. Nevertheless, there is a difference which is most difficult to describe. Some people may not feel it at all, for it is a question of atmosphere and history. Garda was always free from Spanish rule, sheltering under the strong wings of the Lion of St Mark, and this may have given it that air of aloofness which has so often been remarked upon.

Garda has also been called 'mysterious' and I can understand what the writer meant – especially on those rare days of storm when the wind blows from the Dolomites and the jagged ridge of Monte Baldo is wreathed in racing clouds. More austere than the other lakes, there are some who say that it lacks what they like to think of as Italianità – the Italian romance – by which I suppose they mean Baroque villas with marble steps leading down to the water, lush gardens where roses and bougainvillaea riot wantonly over white balustrades, and antique statues glimmering like ghosts in the moonlight. Of course all these things are to be found here in abundance – though not on so luxuriant a scale as in the Land of the Three Lakes. Instead, there is something else – a sterner, almost martial atmosphere. Garda – to Kay and me, at least, carries one back to the Middle Ages. Like that wonderful stretch of the Rhine from Mainz to Cologne, every key-point is crowned by its castle – the grey shells of fortresses built by the Scaligeri of Verona which, when Verona lost her independence, mounted guard for victorious Venice, from Sirmione in the south to the Rocca of Riva and beyond. Maggiore and Como may be attuned to the soft tinkle of mandolins: the mighty mountains of Lake Benacus still seem to echo a flourish of trumpets.

4. Three Smaller Lakes

Lake Lugano

I have called this random chronicle *The Italian Lakes,* but there are so many of them, ranging from the majestic Garda to the little lakes of the Brianza that, even if I had the knowledge, lack of space would not allow me to deal with each of the smaller ones adequately. So I have chosen three, and I am going to begin with Lugano, most of which is Swiss but which Kay and I hold in very special esteem. For us, its very name brings pleasant memories. So, first, a brief diversion, for I would like to describe and thoroughly recommend a rather unusual way of getting there.

Some years ago, we were talking about holidays and one of us said, 'Let's walk over the Alps before we're too old.'

It seemed a good idea but, for some reason, my wife flatly refused to carry a rucksack and calmly announced that, having sent our suitcases on in advance to the hotel in Lugano, she intended to carry her immediate necessities in a perambulator – or, to be more exact, in one of those little push-cars in which very small children ride.

'But, my dear good woman,' I said. 'You can't push a pram over the High Alps.'

'Why not?' she said. 'Hannibal took elephants. Why shouldn't I take a pram?' And she did – probably the first woman ever to do so.

I must admit that 'die push-car', as the porters called it, was a great success and well worth the pound we paid for it. Being made of aluminium, it was light and, when it was stripped, it carried two small cases under a plastic cover. Tied underneath was a length of rope, in case of emergencies. So, while I toiled like Christian under his load of sins, Kay pushed her pram quite easily, while once we were over the top and it was mostly downhill, one finger was enough to steady it.

Our time was limited, so the route we chose was over the St Gotthard Pass, from Wassen to within a mile or two of Bellinzona; and soon after leaving the train, we were walking among pines and little waterfalls, listening to the clonking cow-bells. But we had struck a heat-wave and once we were above the tree-line, a temperature high in the nineties was no joke. So we used to pay our hotel bills at night, a side-door would be left open for us, and we would begin our march at dawn, lying up and resting during the heat of the day. Neither of us will ever forget sunrise over the great peaks or the rosy glow on the mountainsides, which slowly changed from russet to bronze, with apricot light on the snow-patches. Breakfast and luncheon we ate on the road, having so arranged matters that – with luck – we reached an hotel in time for dinner, our one proper meal of the day.

This was Kay's first visit to the Italian Lakes (her great love having been winter sports in the Bernese Oberland) and we could not have chosen a more interesting introduction. What it would be like now I do not know; but even in those days the traffic, though sparse, was our chief hazard. Walking round the loops of those precipice roads gave us some bad moments, though we took every advantage of the old post-paths and, unlike earlier travellers, we had nothing to fear from brigands, bears, or those horrible Alpine vultures, the lämmergeiers, with their 10-foot wing-spread. It was just a pleasant if rather strenuous walk – a succession of crowded days, each of which brought its new experience, and of nights at little mountain inns where, on one occasion, we were entertained by the rousing choruses of the Swiss soldiers, taking their ease after the day's manoeuvres. But most astonishing to us was the abrupt change from German to

Italian scenery and architecture in this country where three cultures meet.

After leaving Wassen we crossed the Devil's Bridge in the spray of a 100-foot waterfall that hurled itself down from the heights. After that, we mounted the long gorge which bears the charming name of the Valley of Horrors – a narrow defile between enormous rocks which rise almost perpendicularly above the brawling, foaming River Reuss. It was hard work in that sweltering heat, but next we had to climb high above the St Gotthard Tunnel to Andermatt and the old village of Hospenthal, with its solitary tower which some say was built by the Lombards. Here the chalets are covered with pinewood slats but, farther on at Faido, the houses are built of solid logs, like an American frontiersman's cabin.

The road spirals on and on – up and up to the bare plateau at the head of the Pass where, as in all very high places, you seem to be on top of the world. There was a hospice here in the fourteenth century, run by Capuchin friars for the benefit of wayfarers; but its successors were destroyed by war, fire, and avalanches, and the present building is an annexe to the big Hospice Hotel where we spent the night. It is an excellent hotel though, of necessity, its appearance is somewhat forbidding. With snow-drifts which can be 30 or 40 feet deep in winter, it was built for strength of plain grey stone and looks as bleak as a prison, looming above a colourless tarn and a memorial of giant bronze birds – eagles or vultures – with outstretched wings. It commemorates brave men who lost their lives here in the Alps.

But it was not long after leaving the Hospice Hotel that we witnessed that dramatic change for, suddenly one morning, we rounded a bend in the road and, there before us like the Promised Lane, was the lovely Val Tremolo, where the Ticino River cascades in a series of waterfalls. Far below us, Airolo and Ambri Piotta – villages quite Italian in character – were shimmering in the heat-haze; we could see grey olive orchards, vineyards, and white churches with campanili; and we knew that, not far away in the blue-green distance, lay Lugano and the Lakes.

Like a last outpost of the wild, there remained the fantastic gorge of the Danzio Grande, with its cataracts and beetling crags. Then, for several days, we followed the Ticino Valley, till gradually the ground began to flatten out, and we were over the Alps. There had not been time to include the foothills but we had walked across the whole of the central massif and, for the first time, we found ourselves looking forward to the comforts of Lugano, to long, lazy days on the Lake steamers, to evenings spent watching a myriad lights twinkling across the dark water, to the clothes that were waiting for us at the hotel, and – to square meals.

When the time came, we appreciated all these things but, delightful as was our stay in Lugano, it will always be overshadowed by the memories of that walk and of the varied incidents which had enlivened our journey: that tremendous Alpine storm which had rocked the Hospice Hotel all night, with the glare of lightning playing on the tarn and silhouetting the spread wings of those sinister birds on the memorial; and the day when I found my dear wife, at crack of dawn, crouching on her heels in the village street of Hospenthal, brewing tea on our little stove and talking bad German to a genial young American motorist – both of them being under the impression that the other was Swiss. Then there was the little cow-herd in the Robin Hood hat, with a rump-stool strapped to his backside, who regaled us with milk warm from the cow in one of the high pastures. And, above all, there was the morning of what we call Kay's Short Cut when, foolishly thinking to save time, we left the road, struck out straight across one of the hairpin bends, and spent about two hours walking half a mile through a clutter of rocks and boggy patches which were invisible from the highway. It was then that we were thankful for the rope for, every 100 yards or so, we had to unload the push-car, lug, pull or push it and its cases up or down boulders to a different level, and then re-load again –

and so ad infinitum. It was during that diversion that I was obliged to ford the infant Reuss with that wretched pram strapped on my back and the water swirling around my bare knees. Kay paddled like a lady.

Now some people have the knack of appearing well turned-out even though the sky should fall, but I cannot say the same for myself. In a cotton frock and a broad-brimmed straw hat which she had bought in Andermatt, Kay would have graced a garden-party – until you looked down at the push-car. But, with my old Army beret, even older corduroys, a short-sleeved green vest, and a rucksack, I must have looked like a member of one of the less reliable Resistance groups. There came an evening when, with an hotel in sight – the only one for miles – Kay gave me a withering glance and said firmly: 'They won't let you in!' So she went on alone to book the room while I mounted guard over our disreputable possessions.

At Lavorgo we entrained for Bellinzona, the ancient key to the St Gotthard, superbly situated with its three castles guarding the Pass. We spent the night there, and the next day were decanted at Lugano, where we trundled our protesting pram over the last lap to our hotel. Except for one blister, we felt very fit, but ready for a long rest in the sunshine. And the heroine of my story? 'Die push-car?' Two nuts were missing and she rattled slightly, but she had served us well. When, years later, the dustmen took her away, it seemed almost a betrayal.

Although it is the smallest of the trinity, there are many who would say that, in the Land of the Three Lakes, Lugano – Lacus Ceresio – is the most beautiful. I cannot go as far as that; but I will agree that, dominated as it is by the three towering peaks of San Salvatore, Monte Brè, and Monte Generoso, it has an intimate charm which is denied to its great neighbours, Maggiore and Como – a charm which even the long, ugly bridge which carries the railway and motor-road across the water from Melide to Bussone cannot destroy.

The greatest length of the Lake – from Agno to Porlezza –

is only 22 miles (14 kilometres) and its greatest width does not exceed 2 miles (3.2 kilometres) while, like all these lakes, it is very deep – in one place nearly 3,281 feet (1,000 metres). Accounts of the North Italian Lakes nearly always include Lugano, for nothing could be more Italian than its architecture and atmosphere, yet a little more than half its area is in the Swiss canton of Ticino: only the north-east arm, the south-east shore between Ponte Tresa and Porto Carésio, and the interesting little enclave of Campione, are Italian.

On the whole, the scenery is more savage and desolate than that of Como or Maggiore – with the exception, that is, of the great Bay of Lugano. On the gentler slopes there are vineyards and orchards; but most of the mountains rise steeply from the water, and there are great gaps between the villages. From the foot of Monte Brè, for example, you look across to the south shore, most of which is virtually uninhabited.

Being almost equidistant from Maggiore and Como, Lugano is an excellent centre for exploration of the whole Lake District except Garda. There are three main basins and a deep, narrow bay called Capolago; but the western arm is almost cut off by the great promontory of San Salvatore, and the shape of the Lake is so irregular and serpentine that it would be almost impossible to take you on another of my 'conducted tours'. As I have said, after our long walk Kay and I were not sorry to take things easily and spend much of our time lazing on the lake steamers, and I am sure that my best plan is to advise you to do the same. So, instead of a methodical exploration of one arm after another, I propose to recommend to you some charming villages, choosing them more or less at random as memory paints pictures of steep arcaded streets slashed with alternate bars of sunlight and shadow, of sudden glimpses of cypress trees like black cut-outs against the glittering water, and of bare peaks reflected in the calm surface of the Lake on which – small as a toy and appearing almost motionless – the steamer is approaching which will carry you home to your hotel.

My advice to you is to do what we did and buy a season

ticket on the boats – for a week, a fortnight, or whatever you will. It is not expensive and it gives you the freedom of the Lake. You can get on or off any steamer just where and when you please, and so retain that liberty which is the essence of a successful holiday. You can plan an expedition to so-and-so, then change your mind and disembark at quite a different village. You can watch the steamer sail without you or, if you are hungry and late for dinner, you can sprint for it along the quay. You can even limp hurriedly with a brave smile, as I did once, in the hope that the vessel will wait for you – a most reprehensible deception which still weighs heavily on my conscience. But even with such a haphazard programme, one must make some attempt to preserve the priorities so it is fitting that I should begin with the ancient town of Lugano, which lies half-way along the north-eastern arm of the lake which bears its name.

At the beginning of the sixteenth century, the Land of the Three Lakes was a stamping-ground for the mercenary armies of Europe in that long-drawn tale of horror which is sometimes called the Italian Wars. I have spoken of these campaigns more than once, so it is enough now to remind you that eventually most of the territory in dispute came under the iron heel of the Hispano-German Emperor. Some few places managed to free themselves from the tyranny of Spain, however – among them the town of Lugano, which the Swiss wrested from the rulers of Milan in 1512. All through the years that followed it resisted every attempt to change its allegiance; and even in 1798, when General Bonaparte destroyed the old Confederacy, it somehow contrived to remain 'free and Swiss'. Until 1881 it shared with Bellinzona and Locarno the honour of taking six-year turns as capital of the new canton of Ticino, but now the cantonal capital remains Bellinzona.

The largest town in the canton, Lugano is situated in a superb position at the mouth of the Cassarate torrent, with Monte Brè and San Salvatore rearing their crests on either side and, two miles away across the water, Italian Campione lying in the shadow of Monte Generoso. If you arrive by train you will have the pleasure of walking out of the station to face a wonderful panorama. Indeed, it is worth coming here by rail if only to enjoy that moment. You will see mountains, range upon range, melting into the far horizon – the nearest, with a bloom like grapes on them, reflected in the calm water.

And right below you, clear-cut as a cameo, lies the old town of Lugano with – almost on your own level – the Cathedral campanile rising above a huddle of ochre- or cream-washed walls and pan-tiled roofs in every shade from pink to russet. Down there are the arcaded streets and the market with its fruit-stalls loaded with oranges and lemons. I remember the oranges and lemons, for they made me wish that I were a painter with the power to capture those gorgeous splashes of colour which glowed in the shadow of the arches. To reach them you must toil down steps – a great many steps, or, if you are as lazy or as wise as I am, you can board the funicular and be carried down to the Cathedral. But if you are lazier or wiser still, you will linger on the station terrace, buy yourself a long, cool beer and sit down in the shade to savour a prospect that you will remember all your days. Lugano is just the place for dawdling. For one thing, it is usually hot. And, for another, it is so beautiful.

At the foot of the funicular but still high above the Lower Town is the Duomo – the cathedral church of San Lorenzo. It contains fourteenth-century frescoes but is chiefly renowned for its Renaissance façade, which experts have placed high among the products of the period. There are three portals surrounded by carving which connoisseurs of church architecture come many miles to see. The one in the centre is said to have been designed by Andrea Bregno, who was born in the lakeside village of Osteno: the other two are by Gaspare Pedoni, who was a townsman of Lugano. But I should also mention that some critics, greatly daring, attribute all three doorways to none other than the great Rodari. It was certainly he who was responsible for the splendid marble and gilt tabernacle which is one of the glories of the church. Kay and I, however, like so many uninstructed visitors, will remember San Lorenzo for its graceful campanile, especially when seen in the foreground of that view from the station terrace.

And now you must go down the hill again to lake level – through narrow cobbled streets of houses with little iron balconies and peeling plaster, to the Piazza della Reforma and the Municipio or Town Hall – a handsome building with a courtyard, by the principal quay for steamers. From there, I suggest that you turn right, along the Riva Vincenzo Vela, and follow it southwards until you come to a symbol of poverty in the midst of plenty – the Franciscan church and convent of Santa Maria degli Angioli.

You will find it down by the waterfront – a long building with a tower, plain to the point of austerity, and now hemmed in and overshadowed by the monster hotels which, we are told, are a sign of progress. You may have doubts about that, so, before you surrender to this heresy, it may be wise to compare this clutter of smart caravanserais which look so alluring on the travel posters with this church and convent which some call mean and ugly. I am not denying that some of the hotels are very good: indeed, I have pleasant memories of staying at one of them when I was young. But for all their slick service and bars and lidi, they fade into insignificance beside St Mary of the Angels in its simplicity and strength. And it is a truism that a plain shell can sometimes conceal a pearl. It is certainly so in this case, for once you have crossed the threshold, this church becomes a shrine of beauty.

You should know that here, in the year 1529, as a guest of the Franciscans, lodged Bernardino Luini, the painter, who was born and spent nearly all his life on the shores of Lake Lugano. In turbulent times he found peace and happiness in the cloisters. He was a guest of the convent for long periods and repaid the brethren's hospitality by adorning their church with several of his masterpieces – his last and, some say, his best. For their greatness we have the evidence of our eyes and the opinion of Jacob Burckhardt, the historian of the Italian Renaissance, who said of this pupil of Leonardo da Vinci that his work was worthy of his master. Could there be higher praise?

So go and see these splendid frescoes, but go on a sunny day, for Santa Maria is even darker than most Italian churches; and if it is dull or late in the afternoon, you may not be able to appreciate the exquisite detail which is half Luini's charm. For example, his huge painting of 'The Passion' on the chancel arch contains no fewer than 150 figures, each beautifully finished. They furnish us with a gallery of cinquecento costume: this is what people really looked like in the days of Ludovico Sforza, Leonardo, and Michelangelo. But that, though interesting, is incidental. The whole great fresco is a noble and most original conception. The Artist's plan was to superimpose the Crucifixion on other incidents of the Passion which, painted on a smaller scale, form an intricate, and effective if somewhat confusing background – confusing, that is, if you are in a hurry, as most people seem to be nowadays. Luini's 'Passion' is a work which repays long and careful study. Some critics say that there are faults (what critics don't?) but even they admit the strength and majesty of the picture – and, above all, the beauty of the kneeling Mary Magdalen at the foot of the Cross. It is hidden beauty, but clear to anyone with imagination, for although she kneels with her back towards us and we can see little of her face except the exquisite curve of a cheek, her glorious golden hair flows down in rippling waves almost to her knees. And that hair tells us everything.

Below the fresco are the figures of St Sebastian and St Roche – the latter, according to tradition, being a self-portrait of the Artist; and these display, not only his mastery of anatomy, but the good sense which refused to make a saint look effeminate. There is a tribute to Luini's master in a superb copy of Leonardo's 'Last Supper', which was removed from the Refectory wall when the building was demolished. And – the favourite with many people – in the right-hand chapel you will find a delightful little lunette or crescent-shaped picture of the Virgin and Child with the young St John. And if, in his 'Passion', Luini showed how he could handle tragedy and a vast panorama, here he displayed his humanity – and dare I say his sense of humour? For the Infant Jesus is playfully pulling the ears of a lamb, while little St John smilingly points to him; and one can even detect the dawn of a laugh in the eyes of Luini's sweet-faced Virgin. This is a real girl and two real children. A lovely little picture.

Coming out of the church into the adjoining Piazza Guglielmo Tell, I advise you to turn back and stroll at your leisure along the Riva to the two principal squares in Lugano: the Piazza Giardino with its gardens and the Piazza Rizziero Rezzonico with its charming fountain. If I were you, I would continue to the Parco Civico, for there you will find a low white villa which is not without interest to those who are thrilled by the highly-coloured romance of the Italian Risorgimento. This house in the Park, built on the site of a medieval castle, is the Villa Ciani. It is now the Historical Museum, but a 100 years ago, it played its part in the long-drawn struggle for Italian freedom and unity. Situated conveniently just across the Swiss frontier, Guiseppe Mazzini – ex-Carbonaro, political agitator, patriot and statesman – made it his headquarters from 1848 until 1866. Here in Lugano were the offices of the clandestine Helvetic Printing Press, which poured out propaganda and revolutionary literature for Mazzini's fellow-countrymen, while at the Villa the Italian–Swiss brothers Ciani held meetings right under the noses of the ostensibly neutral Government of Switzerland. And, for all its air of respectability, one relic of the house's conspiratorial past remains. It is Vincenzo Vela's beautiful statue of a mourning woman, 'La Desolazione', which, according to tradition, had political significance. Surely that can only mean that the sorrowing woman represents Italy in bondage.

One of the places on Lake Lugano which you must on no account miss is Gandria – the last Swiss village on the long eastern arm before you enter Italian waters. I need hardly say that, like all the shores of a lake near a frontier, this district is notorious for smuggling. The *doganieri* are kept on their toes; and at Santa Margherita on the opposite bank there are – or were until recently – strong wire fences on the roads to make life more difficult for those who would 'run' cigarettes, watches, or – worse still – drugs, across a border which, at all times, has been difficult to patrol. Yet, like the old Free Trading in England, it has its lighter side. In her book, *Things Seen on the Italian Lakes,* Mrs Lonsdale Ragg tells the story of the old woman who approached the Customs House after a day's shopping in Lugano Market, accompanied by her grandchildren. On her back she carried one of those high cylindrical baskets called a *gherla* (you can still see them occasionally) and inside the basket, among her other purchases, was an enormous bag of sugar on which duty was payable. Sitting down within sight of the *doganiero,* she carefully divided the sugar into a number of small screws of paper, one of which, with a benevolent smile, she presented to each child. With a cheerful greeting to the Revenue-man, she then hobbled slowly across the boundary into Italy – after which, of course, the 'presents' were returned to her by the 'grand-children'.

To Gandria then! It is an easy walk from Castagnola at the end of the Riva or, if you prefer to do so, you can go by boat from Lugano. You probably know what it looks like already, for it is the quintessence of the picturesque and must have been photographed more often and adorned more calendars than any other place of its size on the Lakes. Gandria, like Morcote at the end of the San Salvatore peninsula, is sometimes referred to as a 'picture postcard' village – and I shall be obliged if you will kindly refrain from wincing at this description. After all, what is wrong in being photogenic? Should one sneer at a village because artists enjoy sketching it? In this enlightened age it is the fashion to be superior about beauty-spots and certainly they attract crowds; but Gandria is not large enough or sophisticated enough to detain the wrong sort of visitor for any length of time. They soon depart in search of vodka martini or 'coke' according to taste, and leave the old place to those who appreciate the outmoded and unpretentious.

But about its picturesqueness there can be no two opinions, for this fishing-village is crammed with what old-fashioned art masters used to call 'bits'. Wherever you set up your easel you will be facing a ready-made composition. Snapped from almost any angle it will yield a rewarding picture. In fact, as a work of art, this conglomeration of houses, set among vines and roses and oleanders, is almost too good to be true. Even the hard-headed road-planners succumbed to the universal sentiment, for when the highway was built which connects Lugano with Menaggio on Lake Como, the engineers' finer feelings prevailed and, at considerable trouble and expense, they drove their new road across the flank of the mountain, leaving Gandria still slumbering peacefully beneath them.

With every inch of space occupied, the village looks for all the world as if it were struggling to retain its foothold on the narrow ledge of rock below Monte Brè to which it clings so precariously. To some extent it resembles pictures that I have seen of hill-villages behind the French Riviera, except that it is not on a hilltop and those who first lived there were in no danger from Barbary corsairs. But the houses are built so close together that, like their Mediterranean counterparts, they seem to be almost under one roof: one man's chimney is only a few feet above his neighbour's tiny yard.

The steep alleys, cobbled and slippery, are nearly all steps – broken, uneven steps down which, as I know to my cost, one must pick one's way with infinite care. Unless you are either very young or have the agility of a goat, when you go to Gandria take a walking-stick. Even so, you will slide and slither through lanes so narrow that, in places, there is only an occasional glimpse of the sky. But the exploration is well worth while; and from the little landing-stage or, better still, from a boat on the Lake, Gandria seen in full sunlight becomes a riot of gorgeous colour. Not only that, but it is one of those 'double' villages that

I have mentioned, and every detail of its houses is reflected in the water.

The little church of Gandria with its miniature campanile looks very old and interesting, but Kay and I did not see it, which was disappointing as I had missed it on a previous visit. When I say that we did not see it, I mean that we did not go inside – and this was the result of our own thoughtlessness and unintentional bad manners.

We were approaching the church door when an aged priest appeared. I am sure that at any other time that white-haired old gentleman, bowed a little with the years, would have looked quite saintly. But that morning he was very angry. Like the angel with the flaming sword, he resolutely barred our way, pointing an accusing finger at Kay as if she were a fallen woman. His rapid speech was almost incomprehensible to us, but gesture never fails an Italian and he soon made his meaning clear. It was a hot day and my wife was wearing a backless sun-frock of which I heartily approved. But not that priest. Oh, no! He did not care for it at all. To him, it was 'fine raiment' worn by a female heretic who would have entered his church improperly dressed.

Now you must have noticed that many people never look funnier than when they are shocked. But I must be fair. It was not so in this case. That white-haired old priest in his shabby soutane did not look funny at all. He was doing what he believed to be right and he maintained his dignity. We were most distressed but all we could do was to apologize as well as we could and turn away disconsolately like Adam and Eve, before the flaming sword of that sharp clerical tongue.

We erred in ignorance and perhaps that old priest was lacking a little in charity; but you must remember that this happened some years ago in a village thronged with tourists who may not all have shared our respect for the Roman Catholic Church. Times have changed; and nowadays we have observed that, in the towns at any rate, Italian priests are more broad-minded and the rules about dress are not so strict. So I mention this

15 *Bergamo: the Colleoni Chapel*

trifling passage-of-arms merely in order that you may be on your guard, for no one would wish to give offence to people so friendly and hospitable.

And now you must make your choice among the villages which lie along the shores of Lake Lugano. Nearly all of them are worth visiting, though I do not think that any of them equal Gandria or Morcote. Of course you may not agree with me; your tastes may be different, so I strongly advise you to trust your luck and take the next steamer to any place that appeals to you. You may find the name attractive: I have discovered wonderful places in England and abroad for no better reason. You may see a picture postcard which you find irresistible. Or a chance conversation with a fellow guest at the hotel may open your eyes to beauties to which Kay and I have been blind.

There is Porlezza at the far north-eastern end of the Lake, from which – across the isthmus and past the lonely little Lake of Piano – one can travel by road to Lake Como. Porlezza, too, has the added attraction of being in Italy. If you have not yet set foot in that country, you may even get a small thrill from your first sight of a member of that famous corps of military police, the Carabinieri – rather naive, perhaps, but one should try not to be too elderly on holiday. And there you will see the flag of Italy – red, white and green, banned during the long years of struggle but now flying freely for all the world to see. The sight of it always reminds me that, once upon a time, patriotic Italian ladies derived a certain satisfaction from being seen at the Opera in a colour scheme on which the most gallant Austrian officer could not possibly compliment them.

Kay has just told me that I have written too much about the Risorgimento. She may be right; but here, in the Land of the Three Lakes, it all seems to have taken place such a short time ago. Perhaps I sounded sentimental with my talk of half-forgotten marching songs and the dancing plumes of the Garibaldini, yet, knowing how she shares my taste for history, I asked her what memories she had already of this, her first visit

16 Verona: Juliet's balcony

to Italy. When she heard the name 'Porlezza', what thoughts came into her mind? Kay thought for a moment, then her answer came: 'An enormous slice of strawberry-and-cream torte. Don't you remember? In that dear little café near the quay.' Perhaps I had better change the subject.

Porlezza then is Italian: I think I have made that abundantly clear. But Ponte Tresa, on the other hand, is a 'double' village in a different sense from Gandria, for the little River Tresa, which flows through it, marks the frontier. On one side of the stream you are in Switzerland: on the other you are in Italy.

Oria we have not visited. Apart from its beauty, its fame rests on the great house which for many years was occupied by the famous novelist, Antonio Fogazzaro, who was the author of several masterpieces and whose *Piccolo Mondo Antico* – translated as *The Patriot* – enjoyed a considerable vogue in England towards the end of the last century. One of Italy's very great men, his house is worthy of his fame. It has been described as 'a villa grappled to the hillside, leaning over the Lake, with its little garden sweet with orange blossom and *olea fragrans.*' From the terrace two lofty cypress trees and an umbrella pine reach up towards the stars; the narrow village street of Oria tunnels humbly beneath house and garden; the Villa Brusati, built in Napoleon's time at the other end of the village, has to yield pride of place to the literary shrine. The very church, adjoining the great house and facing a bronze plaque of the Master, might almost be the private chapel of the Villa Fogazzaro – until we remember where the real power lay, for, in spite of the fact that he was deeply religious, one of his novels, *Il Santo,* was placed on the Vatican Index of forbidden books. So the poor parish priest held the whip-hand over the much-acclaimed best-seller.

And now, at last, it is time to visit Morcote. It is what tourist brochures would call 'a gem' and, like most clichés, that phrase tells the truth although it lacks both restraint and originality. I see in an old diary of mine, written in Lugano, that Kay and I both thought it one of the loveliest and most interesting of the

Lake villages. I should add, perhaps, that for all its beauty, Morcote, at that time, was a rather shabby little place; but more recent photographs suggest that it has been smartened up for visitors. If so, it is a pity.

One of the geographical features which determines the irregular shape of Lake Lugano is the long peninsula which mounts to the imposing heights of San Salvatore; and at the very tip of this wedge of rock, where the two arms of water divide, you will find this village of Morcote which, to me at least, is unique. I suppose that is a bold assertion: 'unique' is a dangerous word. But let it pass, for I have seen no other place of its size which made quite the same impression. Rising through the terraced vineyards at the foot of one of the lesser heights – Monte Arbostora, it is nothing less than a microcosm of medieval and Renaissance Italy. There it is, with hardly a jarring note, preserved for your delight like a fly in amber. Gathered into this tiny compass is a ruined castle, a church with its campanile perched high above the water, and the cypress trees in the near-by cemetery grouped in exactly the right formation from whichever angle you look at them. On the waterfront is a small, arcaded palace which, when we were there, was being used as a bazaar. It looks out on to a tiny piazza; but, best of all, huddled between the mountain and the Lake, is a warren of narrow winding alleys and cobbled steps. To see them you must turn *right* when you land – not left, to the church, as most people do. The atmosphere is quite different from that of Gandria, for there is more of a sense of mystery. Occasionally, in little barred windows set high in otherwise blank walls, you can glimpse a woman's face – instantly withdrawn. Morcote is Swiss but, for some reason, it has a flavour of the East – or, at least, of Barbary. As I told Kay, I had never hoped to be able to show her anything so much like the Kasbah of Algiers.

Here there are infinite possibilities, for Morcote is well worth the attention of the serious author. What a perfect setting for what I might call an intimate historical novel! No fanfaronades, no pomp or pageantry: just the drama of a few ordinary people played out on this small stage. Given the buildings that I have mentioned, the characters would be ready-made and the author would hardly be hampered by the great events of history. Of course I have done no research on the subject; but, although condottieri and their mercenaries marched and counter-marched over the mountains, I would hazard a guess that Morcote has always been off the map. The Visconti, the Sforza, even the Venetians, can have had little time to spare for this small, isolated community. So, by confining the action to a short period, the unities would be preserved, and a writer of the first rank might find material for a masterpiece. As, unfortunately, I shall never rise to those heights, I pass on the notion for what it is worth.

I suppose the most visited building in Morcote is the fine old church of Madonna del Sasso, rising up against the terraced vines as if it had been especially posed for the camera. It contains interesting frescoes, some of which are the work of the school of Leonardo da Vinci; and, within a few yards of the church, is the equally beautiful Campo Santo. This cemetery which, as I have said, is girded with dark cypresses, is a well-known view-point and is itself as photogenic as the church and its belfry against the background of the Lake. Then, on one side of the piazzale, there is the octagonal chapel of Sant' Antonio. And, high above them all, the ruined castle frowns down the hill.

A complete contrast to Morcote is Campione or – to give it its full name – Campione d'Italia. This little Italian enclave was once a fief of the Holy Roman Empire; later, it was a gift from the Emperor to the convent of Sant' Ambrogio in Milan. And so it remained until Candlemas Day in the year 1797, when a commissary of that all-powerful young upstart, General Bonaparte, came marching into the Piazza, followed by two officers in the green uniform of the Cisalpine Legion. In the name of the Sacred People, they planted a Tree of Liberty crowned by a Phrygian Cap – which was a polite way of breaking the news that Campione had been annexed by Revolutionary France. Then, after the fall of Napoleon, the history of the little enclave followed that of Lombardy through the long years of the Risorgimento; and the end of the fight for freedom found its inhabitants firmly Italian – though on excellent terms with their Swiss neighbours. And so they remain.

When you go ashore at Campione there are no Customs formalities and Swiss money may be used. Although I cannot say that I have noticed it myself, some people declare that in the enclave they are immediately aware of a change of atmosphere – in the appearance and speech of the inhabitants, in accent, in verve and gaiety, in the freer use of gesture, and so forth. I am sorry, but I am inclined to attribute this to the visitor's imagination. Campione is Italian all right: if you had any doubt about that, one glance at the tricolour and the patrolling Carabinieri would have convinced you, just as it did at Porlezza. But for hundreds of years Italians and Swiss have lived together in peace and friendship, and there has always been so much intermarriage between the two communities that it is difficult to guess a person's nationality, though no one could *look* more Italian than the loyal Swiss subjects of most of the lakeside villages.

Campione is a delightful little place and must certainly be included in your itinerary. It is no more than a narrow strip of shore, perhaps a mile and a quarter (two kilometres) long, yet it brings a touch of sophistication to what would otherwise be one of the wildest parts of the Lake. You must not expect to find the picturesque but shabby alleys which are so characteristic of places like Gandria and Morcote: Campione has a reputation for gaiety, and for culture going back to the fourteenth century when the 'Maestri Campionesi' became renowned for their church architecture and sculpture. They were the chief master masons of Milan Cathedral, and their work is celebrated in Campione – not only in the parish church and the Oratory of San Pietro (1327) but by the monument in their honour which stands outside Campione's ceramics factory.

The Church of the Annunziata is at the extreme western end of the territory and has many points of interest. Eleven frescoes tell the story of John the Baptist; and, outside the south wall, there are more frescoes under a roof or portico which runs the whole length of the church. There is an elaborate baroque façade and a really magnificent approach from the water. From a little landing-stage flanked by two cypress trees, a double balustraded stairway leads up to the doors, meeting and parting again on four successive landings. If you can approach the church from the water, I would strongly advise you to do so.

But to a great many visitors, the chief attraction of Campione is the Casino which is open all the year round – for here, on Italian soil, a taste for gambling may be gratified to the full in an atmosphere of quiet elegance which must make it almost enjoyable to lose more than you can afford. Being almost invariably unlucky at the tables, I seldom play; but you have three rooms from which to choose, according to the limit that you prefer. There are svelt, poker-faced croupiers who look as if they had been born in evening dress, and, even more worth watching – because, beneath their veneer of sophistication, they are really so pathetic – those compulsive gamblers, male and female, whose whole life seems to centre on the tables. On the Lake outside, men and women on water-skis are foaming along behind their speed-boats; on the lidi, worshippers of the great god Bod are annointing themselves with oil; and on the heights of Monte Generoso, Monte Brè, and San Salvatore, the conquerers of the high tops are reaping their reward by gazing across lakes and mountains into the mists of Italy and trying not to look as if they had come up by funicular. Yet still the devotees sit round the tables – and not only here, but in every casino, large or small, from Monte Carlo to Las Vegas – day after day, night after night, motionless, tensed, listening to the ceaseless song of the sirens – male sirens with expressionless eyes and voices drained of all emotion:

'Faites vos jeux, messieurs et mesdames.'

Lake Iseo

About 25 miles (40 kilometres) to the west of Lake Garda and 10 miles east of Bergamo, lies Lake Iseo – fifth largest of the North Italian Lakes. Easily reached from Bergamo or Brescia, or from Colico at the head of Lake Como, it is little visited by foreigners but has many points of interest, including the largest lake island in Italy. Lake Iseo (Lacus Sabinus) is only 15 miles long and about three miles wide. In some respects, the basin of the Lake resembles Garda, for the surrounding hills become lower and farther apart as you go south; but this great sheet of water is really an expansion of the swift and turbulent River Oglio which flows down the Val Camonica, once famous for the excellence of its arms and armour, and this valley lies between the Bergamesque Alps and the icy massif of the Adamello to the north-east. So Iseo possesses many of the characteristics of an Alpine lake, being less exotic in its general aspect than either Como or Garda. It has been compared to a loch in the Scottish Highlands and one can see the resemblance.

Its history is much the same as that of other parts of Lombardy. Its early inhabitants fiercely resisted occupation by the Romans. The twelfth century saw Barbarossa's mailed horsemen pouring down the Val Camonica, and for the next 300 years there was constant strife. The Visconti of Milan fought the Scaligeri of Verona, while from time to time foreign armies intervened for this cause or that cause or no cause at all, but simply because some lordling was after plunder and liked fighting – until, at last, the troubled countryside found peace for a time under the strong, spreading wings of the Lion of St Mark.

Then in the sixteenth century, when the bad times came again and Venice so cleverly played off her enemies in the League of Cambrai one against another, her most astute move was to release from their allegiance the cities, towns and villages which she held on the mainland. Thus their inhabitants were spared the horrors of the sack and were at liberty to surrender to the overwhelming forces that were brought against them. And they were grateful – the more so when they saw how war was waged by foreign mercenaries. So, as the wily Venetians had foreseen, when the pendulum swung once more in their favour they voluntarily returned to the mild and just rule of the Serene Republic. Among them were the towns and villages round Garda and Iseo; and it was only 300 years later when Venice, in her decrepitude, fell almost without a struggle, that they were all overwhelmed together by the tidal wave of French invasion.

There are four places on the Lake to which I would draw your attention, two in the north and two in the south. Lovere, lying at the foot of Adamello with its white, gleaming peaks, is a pretty little town which yet has important industries; and there are some good pictures to be seen there – both in the parish church of Santa Maria and in the Accademia Tadini, which contains works by Titian, Tintoretto, Giorgione, Paolo, Veronese, and others. Pisogne, too where live men who have inherited and preserved the secrets of the armourers' craft, is worth a visit. But I do not think that either of these places will detain you long.

I would not say the same of the two towns in the south: Sarnico, near which the Oglio River leaves the Lake, and Iseo from which the Lake takes its name – though some authorities have attributed it to the Egyptian goddess Isis, a temple devoted to whose rites stood on the site of the town in the days when Rome, in her decadence, lusted after strange cults.

Sarnico, which possesses a castle and an ancient church, is a pleasant place which owes its prosperity to its silk-weaving industry. But Iseo contrives, quite successfully, to make the best of both worlds, and so may well appeal to visitors with widely differing tastes. On the one hand, it has turned itself into a small conventional resort which lays itself out to please by providing all those things which one associates with small conventional resorts: smart hotels, lidi, water-sports and so on. On the other hand, presided over by yet another statue of Garibaldi, you have an old walled town with a thirteenth-century church – or, rather, the remains of one. Of the original only the campanile, the façade, and the tombs of the Oldofredi family survive; but, above one of the chapel altars is a painting of St Michael which is said to be the masterpiece of the Venetian painter, Francesco Haez – one of the men who introduced the Romantic Movement into Italy.

There can be no doubt, however, that the chief attraction of Lake Iseo is the island of Montisola. Half-way along the Lake and about six miles (9.6 km) in circumference, it dominates the whole scene. There are not many islands which consist of a single mountain, but this one does: moreover, it gave the island its name. And for centuries it has been a place of pilgrimage, for on the summit is a sanctuary – the little church of Madonna della Seriola.

One of the reasons for the romantic and picturesque appearance of Montisola is that in most places the sides of the mountain-island plunge steeply down – nearly 2,000 feet – into the water. This nub of the Lake is guarded by two islets and the ruined castle of the Oldofredi; several villages are strung out along the road which follows the shore, and there are two harbours – Siviano and Peschiera Maraglio. Of these, the latter is the more important. You will find that it is a fine old fishing-village with mellow, red-tiled houses and a multitude of flowers. They seem to be everywhere: in the little gardens, in crannies in the walls, and spilling over the wrought-iron balconies on the quayside, as if to challenge the vivid and variegated colours of the laundry which, like the fishermen's nets, is always hanging out to dry.

Montisola is an ideal retreat for the lover of a quiet life – for all practical purposes cut off from the world, and yet within easy reach of the mainland by means of steamers to other parts of the Lake. For such a one there are several good hotels: indeed, for anybody in search of complete rest and relaxation, Montisola has much to recommend it.

Lake Orta

When Kay and I visited Lake Orta we were without our car; but, thanks once again to C.I.T., that difficulty was soon surmounted. Having made our wants known, a mini-bus appeared and, in the company of four very charming ladies from another hotel, we were able to make the journey from Pallanza in comfort and comparative privacy for, once we had arrived at the town of Orta, we went our several ways, only meeting again for the return journey. No herd. No coach-load of laughing strangers. No loud-mouth guide or amateur humorist. The Compagna Italiana Turismo really is a remarkable organization, for those who run it are blessed with tact and understanding, and respect the wishes of that minority of travellers who value privacy and have not the slightest desire to be 'the life and soul of the party' on holiday or at any other time.

Lake Orta, most of which is in Piedmont, is about eight miles (12.9 kilometres) long and three-quarters of a mile wide, and is separated from Lake Maggiore by the Mottarone massif. There is a funicular from Stresa and, from the summit, it is possible to see seven lakes: Maggiore and Orta, Varese, Mergozzo, Monate, Comabbio, and Biandronno.

Our way lay through Baveno, Stresa and Arona. We stopped for a drink at Arona where, seen at close quarters, the San Carlone – the colossal statue of San Carlo Borromeo – is not only awe-inspiring but slightly sinister. That enormous bronze hand raised in benediction – or could it be admonition? – would be a disquieting thing to live with and, to my mind, the giant effigy serves no useful purpose. It tends to make those of us who are not Roman Catholics forget the saint's self-sacrifice and heroism in time of plague, and remember only the screams of heretics roasting in the Square at Como.

On leaving Arona, we turned westwards along the flank of the Mottarone into wooded hills which, I see from my diary, reminded me of England. This, in spite of passing the Villa

Crespi – built in the Oriental style with a minaret and yet somehow effective. It could so easily have looked like an old-fashioned pier pavilion, but it does not; it blends harmoniously into its alien background. And we were soon brought down to earth again – the earth of medieval Italy, by a fortified tower on a hill, as gaunt and menacing as a Border peel. This is the thirteenth-century watch-tower of Buccione.

The town of Orta which, with the possible exception of Omegna in the north, is the only place of importance on the Lake, lies at the end of a promontory which mounts inland to the Sacro Monte and is just opposite the island of San Giulio – the point on which the interest of the whole lake is centred. The mount, dedicated to St Francis of Assisi, has been turned into a park with trees which delight the arborist. Enclosed by beautiful gates of wood and iron, are 20 chapels, most of which date from the sixteenth or seventeenth centuries, and which contain no fewer than 367 life-sized statues arranged in tableaux representing incidents in the life of the Saint. The summit of the Sacro Monte is crowned by a chapel.

The history of Orta – or Orta San Giulio, to give it its full name – began at the end of the third century, when Theodosius was Emperor. According to the legend, two brothers, Julian and Julius, were sent to preach the Gospel of Christ in the more remote parts of Italy. Julian found his mission field near what is now the town of Gozzano, but Julius (or Giulio) pushed on into the wilds around Lake Cusius, as Orta was then called, little dreaming that this decision of his would make his name immortal.

His imagination was fired by the wooded island in the Lake and he resolved to make it the centre of his ministry. But he met with no encouragement from the local peasantry, who warned him that it was the abode of serpents, dragons, hydras, and other monsters, and was in fact a stronghold of the Powers of Darkness. They flatly refused to row him across to the island but it took more than a few frightened villagers to deter a third-century saint. Doubtless to their surprise, San Giulio spread his cloak on the water and, using his staff as a rudder, sailed across, propelled by a wind which sprang up at exactly the right moment. And if the villagers were surprised, the unclean denizens of the island – dragons, serpents, hydras, and so forth – were even more taken aback. Realizing that their reign was over, they did not even wait for San Giulio to land, but swam for their lives and vanished for ever among the surrounding hills. So the intrepid saint took possession of the island and, like many another anchorite, lived for some years in a little cell which he built with his own hands. And that humble hut was the beginning of the great mass of building which, nowadays, covers the once-wooded island from shore to shore.

Moving out of the realm of legend into the Dark Ages of history, we find that, in the year 575, Mernulphus, lord of the island, was beheaded for treachery by Agilulf, King of the Lombards, whom we have met before as husband of the peerless Theodolinda. A white marble sarcophagus, near the door of the Basilica and now used as an alms-box, is said to have held his bones. Certainly, when it was discovered in the late seventeenth century, it contained a headless skeleton, and the letters 'M.E.R.N.U.L. . . .' can still be deciphered.

Another event in the distant past was the heroic defence of the island in 962 by Willa, wife of Berengar, another King of the Lombards, against the powerful army of the Emperor Otho the Great.

On that golden summer day, Kay and I could have wished for more time but, even so, we had leisure to explore both the town and the island. The place grows on you; and, when we are talking about the Lakes nowadays, the conversation nearly always turns to Orta. It is very quiet, and while we were there we saw nothing which even remotely suggested synthetic gaiety. But we shall never forget the almost indescribable atmosphere of peace and tranquility. We found nothing to equal it in Italy. Hardly a ripple ruffled the surface of the water in which Isola di San

Giulio was mirrored, and there was a heat-wave which made everything seem slightly unreal except in the deep shadow or in the brooding silence of the churches.

There is not too much to see in Orta – and perhaps that was just as well, for it was one of those days known to all travellers when, faced with interminable art galleries or with monuments of antiquity which, most unfeelingly, the Goths, the Huns and the Vandals failed to destroy, the average Englishman on the Continent longs for libations of wine or – in my case, as I do not greatly care for wine – for enormous draughts of ice-cold beer. And, that day, the beer was not only forthcoming but worthy of the occasion – at a cool, arcaded hotel by the shore, which I can thoroughly recommend. In the seventeenth century it was a convent: nowadays, there must be many strangers who are thankful for its hospitality and for the friendly manager whose knowledge of our language added so much to our enjoyment.

The town of Orta really consists of one main street, picturesque with iron balconies and made beautiful with flowers; but there are a number of side lanes and alleys, and alleys are nearly always rewarding, in Italy or anywhere else. The little quay from which you cross to the island adjoins the shady Piazza Motta – a small square dominated by the Palazzo Comunale. This is a beautiful little building dating from 1582. It is set high above a portico, with an outside stair, frescoed walls, and a miniature campanile. But there are also a number of interesting sixteenth-century private houses, especially in the Piazza and in the Via Vaire Albertolli. These include the Casa Giani, the Palazzo Gemelli with its sculptured doorway, and the Casa Margaroni which, for some reason, is called the House of the Gnomes. I scented a story here but unfortunately I was never able to unearth it.

After a leisurely stroll through the streets, we mounted the flight of steps which leads up to the portico and marble doorway of Santa Maria Assunta. Very light and airy for an Italian church, it was built in the form of a Latin cross, with a cupola over the transept crossing. It is said to have been rebuilt in the eighteenth century on the site of a much earlier church, some parts of which still remain. The doorway by which we entered dates from the eleventh century and there is a magnificent Romanesque ambo or pulpit that is 200 or 300 years older. Made of marble, it displays in high relief the symbols of the Four Evangelists: the Winged Man of St Matthew, the Winged Lion of St Mark, the Winged Ox of St Luke, and the Eagle of St John. A most remarkable piece of work which carries one straight back to the Dark Ages. But we were going to see an even finer example of carving which made us think of the Vikings for, after leaving the church, Kay and I crossed over to the Isola di San Giulio – 'the gem-like island', as John Addington Symonds called it.

By the landing-stage there were several small motor-boats to take people to the island though, except for ourselves and a solitary boatman, the little quay was deserted. When we reached the other side we saw more of these boats ready to ferry passengers back to the mainland; but, as we crossed the narrow strip of water, John Addington Symond's vision began to fade. Some people might agree that the island is 'gem-like', for certainly there is colour: we could see clumps of trees and small gardens gay with roses and oleanders. But our prevailing impression was of one solid mass of masonry, of buildings piled almost on top of each other as they rose from the water's edge to the campanile of the Basilica and the enormous seminary which, in 1840, was built on the site of an ancient fortress. We remembered that this island was – and, indeed, is – of an importance out of all proportion to its size for, all through the nineteenth century, the Lake of Orta was ruled from the Isola di San Giulio. These buildings had included not only the principal church, but the cemetery, what was then the Town Hall, and a number of villas owned by the aristocracy of Milan. A queer, impressive, brooding place that seemed to have grabbed every inch of land – from the huge bulk of the seminary with its rows of little black windows to the narrow road – or, rather, pathway – that skirted the shore. And presently it began to dawn upon us that we were having a strange experience – though it may only have seemed strange to us at the time because, at the back of our minds, were those sinister legends of the island's past, before the Saint rescued it from the Powers of Darkness. You can put it all down to imagination: I am sure that is the truth. You can believe any explanation you choose. But the fact itself cannot be denied.

What was this fact? Something very simple. As we strolled along, it was gradually borne upon us that the place seemed to be deserted. At any rate, it was deserted as far as we were concerned. No doubt eyes were watching us from those rows of blank windows. No doubt if we went there tomorrow or next week we would find San Giulio thronged with people. We may have arrived at an awkward hour when the inhabitants had departed 'en masse' for some religious ceremony or civic junketing of which we knew nothing. The fact remains that Kay and I were on that island for some considerable time and met no living soul – no one at all. Road, landing-stage and church were alike deserted. There must have been at least one shop or café but neither of us can remember seeing either. It reminded us of books we have read about those abandoned Maya towns deep in the jungles of Yucatan.

Still alone (the sight of a friendly dragon or hydra would have been almost welcome!), we made our way into the Basilica, said to be the most important Romanesque building in the province. Begun in the fourth century, on the site of the original anchorite's cell, and restored on several occasions from the ninth to the eighteenth century, it was built on much the same plan as Santa Maria Assunta. There are a number of frescoes – the best by Gaudenzio Ferrara, and some singularly beautiful choir-stalls of black polished walnut, while there is preserved a relic of more credulous times in the shape of the fossilized vertebra of a whale. I need hardly say that this was thought to be part of one of the fabulous monsters which formerly terrorized the island. There are also a number of graffiti which provide food for thought. Nowadays, anyone who scratched his name or a message on the wall of a church would rightly be denounced as a vandal. Yet these medieval scribblings – these records of pilgrimages, floods and plagues, are solemnly studied by antiquarians and given an honoured place in the guide-books. It is a strange world.

But here on the island, the glory of the church is again the marble pulpit which, in this case, dates from the eighth or ninth century. It is difficult to realize that it was not fashioned in Scandinavia, for here we see, worked in marble, the intricate knots and interlaced strappings which are characteristic of Norse wood-carving of the time and redolent of longships and the stave-churches of Norway. On this wonderful old pulpit there are both Christian and pagan symbols and you can see a whole array of legendary monsters – including a satyr with a bow-and-arrow who is about to attack a griffin and crocodile while they are settling a little difference as to which of them should devour an unfortunate goat. For a few moments those creatures of the dawn seemed very real.

It is only a short distance from the church to the landing-stage, and Kay and I had plenty to think about. We had enjoyed our visit to the island and now we were quite ready to board a boat which would carry us back to Orta.

But the boats had all gone.

And now, as I am trying to tell the truth, I must reluctantly record a rather ridiculous anti-climax. As I have said, every boat had disappeared – we could not imagine why – and there we were, more or less marooned on the legendary island which, to us that day, was about as 'desert' as a desert island can be. There was not a single person in sight to help us out of our difficulty; and although, across the water, we could just see our white car waiting on the Piazza Motta, we could not help wondering how long it would remain there. Obviously it could not do so indefinitely, and neither our driver nor our fellow passengers knew that we had crossed to the island.

Somehow we had to find transport across that narrow strip

of water. It was all very well for San Giulio to use his cloak for a raft, but somehow I did not think that my sports-coat would prove as useful. All that we lesser mortals could do was to wave Kay's scarf and a handkerchief tied to my stick. We did that for quite a long time without the slightest response; and, although I have been told that I have a powerful voice, my shouts went unanswered – both from the mainland and from the great mass of buildings behind us.

I suppose we waited on that deserted landing-stage for about three-quarters of an hour, although it seemed longer – much longer, and we never did discover who missed us in the end. But at last, after having had our hopes dashed several times, we saw a motor-boat detach itself from the little quay at Orta and – yes! – this one really was coming across to the island. So if you go to Orta you should certainly not miss the Isola di San Giulio. But, unless you are one of those peculiar people with a Crusoe complex, take my advice and make sure that the boatman understands that you are booking a two-way passage.

There are several villages round the shores of Lake Orta, but we returned to Pallanza by way of Omegna, which is an interesting old town at the northern end of the Lake. The medieval walls have gone but there are still some old houses, a fine old church – Sant' Ambrogio – a bridge built by the Sforza of Milan, and one of the town gates, the Porta Castello, which leads to a narrow, winding glen called the Valle Strona which, I understand, is popular with walkers. But, nowadays, Omegna is a small commercial and industrial town and I do not think that we lost a great deal by having to hurry through it. Yet, on second thoughts, I would correct that statement, for anyone is the loser who has to hurry through any part of this delectable little lake.

As you will have guessed, Kay and I fell in love with Orta, for it has something which we have not discovered elsewhere in Italy – or in England either, for that matter. If I were trying to write whimsy, I would call it the Place Where Time Stands Still, but I lack the genius of the late Sir James Barrie, so please forget it. Nevertheless, the title would not be entirely untrue. The time may come when bright businessmen will disfigure its shores with high-rise flats and hideous hotels. Leering young ladies with too little on may beckon you there from the brochures. But that time has not come yet.

It may have been the magic of that glorious summer day – the peace, the silence, the serenity. But in that lovely old town and on the island we could forget the troubled times in which we live. We would like to go there again.

5. Three Near-by cities

Milan

And now, in the limited space at my disposal, I would like to write about three famous cities, all within easy reach of the Lakes and all very well worth visiting. Indeed, most people who go to the Lakes make a point of including one or more of them in their itinerary. The three that I have chosen are Milan, Bergamo and Verona. Perhaps I was wrong to omit Brescia, but I preferred to concentrate on those which, to me, are the most interesting.

First, to Milan then, which lies in the very heart of the Plain of Lombardy. It is the second city of Italy, the wealthiest commercial and industrial centre, the seat of an archbishopric, a great railway junction, and the headquarters of an army corps; and yet, in the words of Mr H. V. Morton, it 'has always been one of those cities visited on the way to somewhere else'.

This is certainly so in my case. I was not there for long and Kay was not with me, so I did not have the advantage of her advice and criticism. But I hope that, at least, I shall be able to set up some sign-posts which will point the way to interesting discoveries. They are there to be made; but, in many cases, they are hidden and if, like mine, your taste is for the old and the picturesque (and surely it must be if you have got so far with this book!) you will have to prowl about this vast metropolis with its tower blocks and factories until some strange or beautiful survival rewards your patience and crowns your day.

So take heart! And please remember that the element of

contrast will always be there to surprise you. Milan is noisy, even for Italy, yet for all the roar of the Stock Market and the unholy din of the traffic, there are quiet gardens in the heart of the city where, through noble gates of wrought iron, you can see green lawns, statuary, and cool fountains; the place is notorious for the violence of its riots and public protests, yet there is a civic pride and local patriotism which other urban populations might do well to emulate; and, while the assembly lines are pouring out their cars and typewriters and armaments, Milan is still one of the world's leaders in music and the arts.

The earliest settlement on this site – already an important centre before the Roman conquest, fell to the irresistible legions in the third century B.C., and just over 400 years later, when it had ousted Rome itself as the seat of government of the Western Empire, Milan ensured its place in world history, for it was here, in A.D. 313, that the Constantine Edict was proclaimed which ended the persecution of the Christians. Their new position of power was consolidated by the work of a remarkable succession of bishops. They were militant churchmen and statesmen; and among them was St Ambrose, one of the four Latin doctors of the Church and an outstanding figure in the Dark Ages.

In the course of this book I have used that phrase several times for the very good reason that I could think of none better. And if it is a cliché, it is also an accurate description, for those days really were dark – and nowhere more so than in Italy. With the eruption of barbarian hordes from the steppes and deserts of Central Asia, their slow sweep westward spread a pall of horror and despair over Europe. In the year 452 Milan was sacked by Attila and his Huns, and they were followed by the Goths and by the Langobards who were to give Lombardy its name. All the terrors of the Apocalypse seemed to have been let loose on a sinful world, but the wheel kept on turning – slowly – very slowly. The devastation lessened and out of chaos emerged the brave new world of the Middle Ages.

To the people of Milan the Middle Ages and the Renaissance

meant rule by one of two great families: the Visconti and their successors, the powerful House of Sforza. The humanist culture of the city states was followed by a revival of learning and the arts unequalled since the days of the Greeks, and nowhere did it flourish in finer flower than in Milan. But after the great days came domination by the Spaniards and Austrians, and this went on for hundreds of years, with a short interval when the all-conquering General Bonaparte made Milan the capital of his puppet state, the so-called Cisalpine Republic. After his downfall the Austrians returned and remained in occupation until the union with Piedmont. Soon after, Milan became part of the Kingdom of Italy; but let us turn back the pages of history to the late fourteenth century, when Gian Galeazzo Visconti carved out a dukedom and gave his city the huge church which is one of the wonders of the world. And just as Milan lies in the heart of Lombardy, so in the heart of Milan – in almost the exact centre – you will find this fantastic cathedral. It is the third largest church in Europe, yielding pride of place only to St Peter's in Rome and the Cathedral of Seville.

The building, begun in 1386, is for the most part a miracle of Northern Gothic and is the work of a succession of architects and masons: Frenchmen, Germans, Italians – including the Maestri Campionesi from the Lake of Lugano. Built of 'sarizzo Ghiadone', a stone resembling granite, it is faced throughout with white marble. The Cathedral was consecrated in 1577 by Carlo Borromeo, now Archbishop of Milan, but it cannot be said that it was finished – if it ever has been finished – until 1897, when the great doors were hung in place.

Walk round the outside and marvel at the rich fretting and the forest of pinnacles and flying buttresses. More than one optimist has tried to count the statues but I cannot be sure that any two of them have ever agreed. The number is somewhere near 2,300 – give or take a saint or two either way – and there are about 2,000 more inside. Then there are 135 pinnacles and, high above them, reaching to a height of 354 feet, a richly fretted tower containing a gilded statue of the Virgin – familiarly but not irreverently known as La Madonnina and beloved by all true Milanesi.

Note the three stained glass windows in the polygonal apse: they are said to be the largest in the world. You will note also, I am afraid, the incongruity of the façade. The baroque porches, though excellent in themselves, were built later and are out of key with the Gothic grandeur which is so impressive.

Go inside. At first you will be overwhelmed by the sheer majesty of the interior and your only desire will be to stand and stare – or, rather, peer almost fearfully into the gloom, for the mighty cathedral is enveloped in a mysterious dusk through which loom gigantic pillars, soaring up into the darkness. You will see the tiny glimmerings of votive candles, but only when your eyes have become accustomed to the change from the bright sunlight outside will you begin to discover the many treasures which this vast building enshrines. I can mention only a few.

First you will surely want to examine more closely those splendid stained glass windows. Some of them date from the fifteenth century and very splendid they are; but, in fairness, I must tell you that they were renovated and partly re-made just over a 100 years ago.

Then there is a magnificent bronze candelabrum, the base of which was made by Frenchmen in the thirteenth century: it is in the form of a tree with seven branches. You will see, too, Leoni's tomb of Giacomo de' Medici, Marquis of Marignano and brother of Pope Pius IV. It is of white Carrara marble, adorned with two black and two white columns which were a gift from His Holiness, and two taller pillars of a variegated stone which is very like jasper.

The cathedral choir is in the presbytery, and in the crypt beneath lie the remains of San Carlo Borromeo in a crystal sarcophagus. If you wish, you can join the queue which is ushered down the stairs for a closer inspection of the body of this very great man, now reduced to a skeleton – masked, gloved, and in full canonicals. As a contrast to the overpowering colossus that looms above Arona, it is pathetic and rather terrible. That is why I would not care to go down to that crypt. I am no friend of heretic-hunters, but San Carlo did his duty as he saw it. And how many of us can say as much? I feel that his bones should be left in peace, for I doubt if many of the sightseers are impelled by genuine religious motives. To the few I offer my apologies, but I maintain that this man deserved a better fate than to have his remains gaped at by a shuffling queue of trippers.

And then, if you would sup full of horrors, in the south transept there is a statue of St Bartholomew who, according to tradition, suffered martyrdom by being skinned alive in Armenia. He carried his skin thrown over one shoulder like a cloak, and the sculptor's rendering of every muscle and tendon in the poor flayed body is masterly. I am told that the sight of such things deepens the reverence of a devout Roman Catholic; but, as you may have guessed, I have an aversion to these grisly exhibits so, unless you have a more fully developed sense of the macabre than I have, I suggest that you hurry up to the roof, where a really marvellous experience awaits you.

The door is in a corner of the south transept and you will find yourself faced by 158 steps, so take my advice and go by lift. Apart from the tower which enthrones the Madonnina, the roof is on two levels connected by steps which follow the flying buttresses, and once you emerge into the sunlight you are in a different world. You climb from one terrace to the other, and all around you is what appears to be a petrified forest of stone. Statues and pinnacles, dozens of them – with, in between, fascinating glimpses of the Square and roofs of Milan. Miniature cars crawl past the arcades, where people like busy dolls are going about their lawful occasions, while high among the chimney-pots, among the fluttering lines of washing in the tiny roof-gardens, move others – unaware of or indifferent to the fact that they can be seen from the Cathedral.

And where, at last, the houses end your eyes can travel across the whole expanse of the Plain of Lombardy – green with crops and criss-crossed by those lines of pollarded mulberry trees which feed the silkworms of Como; and farther still, if you are lucky, you may be rewarded by a sight of the dim ramparts of the Alps. The Château of Chambord on the Loire is justly renowned for its roofscapes. I am told that you can open a door between two chimney-stacks and step out into what appears to be a blue-and-white town of stone and slate, of turrets, cupolas, and pavilions. But I am sure that the prospect from the French château cannot compare with that which Milan Cathedral has to offer. If the roofs of Chambord are like a town in the air, this is a city of white marble.

The great square in front of the Cathedral is the Piazza del Duomo. Except for the perimeter, it is mercifully free from traffic – a vast expanse of variegated pavement in a city where, as in most cities, an open space in which one can escape from motor-cars is a most desirable oasis. On two sides are the 'portici' or arcades where the Milanesi love to linger, while at the west end, facing the Cathedral, is an equestrian statue of King Vittorio Emanuele II. It is a fine piece of work by Ercole Rosa, and I seem to remember that His Majesty is not flourishing his sabre or looking quite as warlike as usual.

The Piazza del Duomo really is the centre of the city, in the sense that it is the best starting-point for all the other places of interest; but here in the square itself are two great palaces: the residence of the Archbishop and the former Palazzo Reale. The latter is a comparatively modern building (1772) but it stands on the site of an older mansion which, in its time, was occupied by both the Visconti and the Sforza. Their private chapel still survives as the ancient church of San Gottardo: and if you walk for a little way down the Via del Palazzo Reale, you can see its apse and singularly beautiful campanile. It was in this church that, in 1412, that revolting young sadist, Giovanni Maria Visconti, was assassinated for his sins.

These palaces are both on the south side of the square, while on the north side is the famous Galleria Vittorio Emanuele – a glass-roofed arcade in which are some of the best shops, restaurants and cafés in the city. But this, too, is haunted by tragedy for its designer, Guiseppe Mengoni, fell to his death here on the day before that fixed for the official opening in 1878. And if you are in the mood for smart shops and bars, try the Via Dante which runs from the Piazza de' Mercati to the Public Park, or the Via Monte Napoleone, which you can reach by going northwards from the Cathedral along the Via Alessandro Manzoni. They are considered some of the finest streets in fashionable Milan.

There are, of course, many churches worthy of a more detailed description than I could afford in this short account of the city, in which so much had been sacrificed (I believe, rightly) to the Cathedral. The most important is undoubtedly the Ambrosian Basilica, which one writer found cold and dark, but which another described as the most beautiful church in Lombardy. It is certainly one of the most interesting, for it was founded in the year 386 by the saint who, by his strength and wisdom, made possible the Milan that we know, and whose revered bones now rest in a crypt beneath the high altar. If ever a man deserved well of the Milanesi it was St Ambrose.

It was here in Sant' Ambrogio that the old Germanic and Lombard kings and emperors, having taken their oath by the coronation pillar, were crowned with that most sacred of diadems, the Iron Crown of Lombardy, which holds within its golden circlet an iron nail from the Cross of Christ. Although it was founded in the fourth century, the church bears all the characteristics of the eleventh and twelfth, when the extensive alterations took place which made it one of the most famous medieval monuments in Italy. You should ask to be taken to see the altar – a marvellous example of repoussé work in gold and silver, enriched by Byzantine enamel of the ninth century.

You reach Sant' Ambrogio by going westwards from the Piazza del Duomo. Follow the Via Torino as far as the Corso di Porta Ticinese; and then, as you have to bear round to your right past the Military Hospital, I would suggest that you ask your way. It is not far. But asking your way in Italy is always worth while, if only because it affords you yet another example of the kindness and courtesy of your hosts.

Milan's oldest church is San Lorenzo Maggiore, in which you can see mosaics which date from the fourth century. Then there is Sant' Eustorgio, just outside the Ticinese Gate – where, incidentally, the sixteen Corinthian columns are Roman – and this contains the Portinari Chapel, which has been described as 'a perfect jewel in stone'. And you will be interested in the little Renaissance church of San Satiro, built by Bramante in 1480, the charm of which lies in the fact that although it is really quite small, by some miracle of perspective it has been made to appear spacious.

Most visitors to Milan, having seen the Cathedral, hurry on to the Dominican church of Santa Maria delle Grazie. It is a beautiful building of brick and terracotta; but the attraction to the average tourist is not in the church itself but in the building which adjoins it. For here, to the left of the façade, is the Refectory of the Dominicans and all that remains of one of the most famous paintings in the world – Leonardo da Vinci's 'Last Supper' – 'Il Cenacolo', as the Italians call it.

This great picture has recently been restored as effectively as it can be, but perfect restoration is out of the question. By the middle of the sixteenth century it had begun to deteriorate, the colours flaking and scaling, and crusts of mildew appearing, caused by the damp walls of the Refectory. The painting had been executed in tempera, which is inferior to true fresco in durability, and several attempts at restoration were made during the eighteenth century in the mistaken belief that the picture had been painted in oils. No really effective measures have ever been taken – or, perhaps, could ever be taken – to counteract the damp, and there have been other calamities. In the seventeenth century the friars knocked a doorway through it in order to speed the passage of their food from the Kitchen to the Refectory; during the Napoleonic Wars, French soldiers (and their horses) were quartered in the building; and the picture sustained further damage when Milan was bombarded during the Second World War.

Always afire with some new project and driven by some force within him, it was Leonardo's tragedy – as it is ours – that so much of his work was left unfinished. 'The Last Supper' was no exception – though for a different reason. The moment chosen in the Divine Drama was that in which Jesus said 'One of you will betray me.' The picture shows the reaction of the Disciples, and into the painting of their faces, the Artist put all his skill and all his knowledge of human nature. So when he came to paint the face of Christ Himself, he had no reserve of power or beauty with which to depict the Son of God at this supreme moment of history. Faced with this tremendous challenge, he left the face unfinished. As Vasari says, '. . . feeling that he could not give it that celestial divinity which it demanded.' It has always seemed to me that those who call Leonardo an atheist should remember this story of the humility of one of the greatest and most versatile geniuses that the world has ever known.

Leonardo da Vinci. Artist, architect, pageant-master, military engineer, musician, mechanician, philosopher, and – above all – student of Nature. Those who are interested in this marvellous man would be well advised to go straight from his most famous picture to the most interesting museum in Milan – the Museum of Science and Technology. It is in the Via Zenale, quite near Santa Maria delle Grazie; and in it you can see, constructed from his own notes, working models of Leonardo's inventions. Many years in advance of his own time, they include the armoured tank, diving-gear, and the flying-machine that so nearly flew. If only he had known the power of petrol, what might he not have achieved. And yet perhaps it was as well that this knowledge was withheld from him: the Western World enjoyed several more quiet centuries free from what many regard, not without reason, as one of the curses of mankind. But one stands abashed before the stupendous scope of this man's intellect and achievements. Such supreme skill in so many branches of art and science! Such curiosity about every aspect of the world in which he lived! And, hindering all, that one weakness – a Daemon who drove him so relentlessly that each new idea crowded out the last before it had reached consummation.

And what else is there to see in Milan? Enough to occupy you for weeks. But if, as I imagine, your time is limited, you will have to make your own selection which should, if possible, include the Ambrosian Library, the Pinecotaca or Picture Gallery in the Palazzo di Brera – a fine collection of Italian paintings, and, above all, the Castello Sforzesco and La Scala Opera House.

The great red stronghold of the Sforza lords lies north-west of the Piazza del Duomo in another open square. It was built to replace the Visconti castle which the ever-turbulent mob of Milan demolished in 1447. The architects were Bramante, Filarete and Leonardo da Vinci, and it was based on three massive towers. The central one – the Torrione del Filarete – is a modern reproduction, the original having been destroyed by an explosion of gunpowder struck by lightning. The castle has been used as a barracks by the various armies which, at different times, have occupied Milan; but now it is open to the public and you may wander through the marble halls where Il Moro's condottieri clanked in their Milan plate, and where his adorable wife, Beatrice d'Este, spent her all too short married life. In the Corte Ducale there is a magnificent collection of sculptures and paintings, and the castle houses a priceless exhibition of Chinese and Japanese art dating from 300 B.C.

And, lastly, I hope that you will be able to spend an unforgettable evening at La Scala. It is not easy to buy tickets but you may be lucky. Starting as usual from the Cathedral but, this time, going north along the Galleria Vittorio Emanuele, you come to the Piazza della Scala and the opera house which, with the exception of the San Carlo in Naples, is the largest theatre in Europe. It was built in 1778 on the site of a church which had been endowed by Beatrice della Scala, wife of Bernabo

Visconti, and there were those who foretold that no good would come of this profanation of hallowed ground. It is true that La Scala has had its misfortunes; but, judging by the box-office returns, it is to be hoped that the sin – if it was a sin – has been forgiven. During World War Two the Scala was completely destroyed by Allied bombing, and it is pleasant to remember that the Allies contributed generously towards its reconstruction. The new opera house is an exact replica of the old and its formal re-opening by Arturo Toscanini took place in 1946.

The theatre, which can seat over 3,000, is surrounded by tiers of boxes and the auditorium is lighted by magnificent chandeliers. The enormous stage will accommodate a chorus of 100 and the orchestra consists of about the same number of musicians. Sixteen operas are presented each season, which lasts from December until June, with a further short run in July.

Attached to La Scala is the Theatrical Museum where, in addition to exhibits recalling the theatres of Ancient Greece and Rome, there is a fine collection of Sicilian puppets and one room devoted to the Commedia dell' Arte. Here, if anywhere outside Venice, one can recapture the fascinating but rather sinister atmosphere of the *improvisatori* – Pierrot, Columbine, Harlequin, Scaramouche with his cock's feather, and the villainous Polichinello.

Bergamo

It was while we were staying in Bellagio that we visited Bergamo, and again the ubiquitous C.I.T. proved our friend. Kay, who is the practical member of our partnership and our highly efficient transport officer, made a few inquiries at our hotel, with the result that we went in a hired car driven by a big, handsome Neapolitan with a jet-black moustache that lengthened above very white teeth when he smiled – which he did most of the time. His few words of English were a joy; and he was a magnificent driver with whom somehow one felt safe when he touched 90 m.p.h. – and even when, while rounding a hairpin bend, he took both hands off the wheel to gesticulate and blow ecstatic little kisses into the air, like a foreign 'chef' recommending some dish in a TV commercial. He was describing his favourite meal: 'Spa-ghett-i and tom-ay-ti with plenty o-il! Aha! Beautiful!' He was a character.

He drove us up the Lecco Arm of Lake Como, past the High Brianzo and Lecco, where we crossed that medieval bridge built by the Visconti. The country beyond the town is industrial too and rather uninteresting, so an old watch-tower on a hill looked forlorn and out of place – which only shows how foolish a man with a pen in his hand can become. For why in the world should I have written such nonsense? Why in the world, on the hotel terrace that night, should I have noted down – gravely and in all sincerity – that a peaceful if dull countryside devoted, in the main, to the harmless manufacture of silk, where men can live useful lives and die at last peacefully in their beds, should somehow be less interesting than that same plain a few hundred years ago, when the watch-tower served a useful purpose in a land devastated by war?

I was going to cut the above passage but I prefer to let it stand, if only to show how, even among peaceable people like myself, some old-fashioned notions of what used to be called 'romance' can die hard – as difficult to grub out as bindweed and just as deadly. But the next note I made that evening, under the vines at Bellagio, was more sensible and more worthy of the dignity of print, for I see that it tells how, all at once, we came in sight of Bergamo, with its domes and roofs and towers, riding its rocky ridge like a coloured cut-out – the one solid thing in a realm of air and misty distances. At that time and in that place, we both thought it even more dramatic than the famous prospect of Edinburgh – and as my wife is half Scots, that is quite an admission.

There are really two Bergamos – the Città Alto in its old Venetian walls, high on the hill; and the Città Bassa, a big manufacuring town (textiles) which, with its suburbs, occupies the lower ground. The latter has some fine modern buildings, including the Sports Stadium, and its present prosperity matches the impregnability which was once the boast of the Old City.

Situated at the junction of two rivers, the Brembo and the Serio, Bergamo is one of the most interesting cities in Lombardy but it is not visited by tourists nearly as much as it deserves. It has a stirring history and, for a place of its size, more than its fair share of famous men, including the composer, Donizetti, who has a museum devoted to him and his works; Lorenzo Lotto, the painter; and that most formidable condottiere, Bartolomeo Colleoni.

From ancient times, when the once Roman Bergomum became the centre of a Lombard duchy, it shared the common experience of serving as shuttlecock in that dangerous game which was for ever being played by the Italian tyrants, until the City Fathers had the good sense to place themselves and their town under the protection of Venice. Then at last, in 1797, when the Serenissima fell to Bonaparte, the bad times came for Bergamo as for the rest of Italy. Waterloo brought no respite, for the Austrians were in the saddle; but when, during that same nineteenth century, the nation stirred in its sleep and then slowly awoke, the old town on the hill was ready to play a glorious part. Of the immortal Thousand who landed with Garibaldi in Sicily, the largest contingent – 180 volunteers – came from Bergamo, and so earned their native town the proud title of Città dei Mille. It was here, too, that the Battle Hymn of the Garibaldini was sung for the first time.

For those who have no car there is a funicular to the Upper Town – the City of Silence as it is sometimes called. And it has been well named, for comparatively silent it is – blessedly so to those whose eardrums have been assailed by the traffic noises of an Italian city. Unlike coaches, cars are not absolutely banned, for we found ourselves following the steep road which encircles the rock and made our entrance through one of the ancient gateways; but, once inside the walls, the wise motorist studies humility, accepts that here he is a second-class citizen, and minds his P's and Q's.

Let us suppose that you have entered Bergamo Alta by the Porta Sant' Agostina. You should follow the Via Dipinta, pausing to have a look at the thirteenth-century church of San Michele al Pozzo Bianco, where there are some frescoes by Lorenzo Lotto. The narrow and picturesque Via Gombito will then take you past the tower of that name – grim, grey, and almost windowless, to the Piazza Vecchia, which is the heart of Old Bergamo.

I believe I am right in saying that, once you have been comfortably installed at one of the café tables, you will ever afterwards join me in telling people that, for anyone who loves Italy, Bergamo is a 'must'. In this book (and elsewhere) I have written a lot about the past – perhaps too much. But, remembering the Piazza Vecchia, I regret nothing: I refuse to retract a word. It has been described as one of the most beautiful squares in the world; and, not having been all over the world, I can neither confirm nor deny it. But I do say this. If you are interested in medieval Italy, here it is all around you – an empty stage waiting for the players: men in velvet and steel and parti-coloured hose, leggy boys with clubbed hair, and willowy girls in long gowns who made their exit centuries ago, leaving the stage on which they once strutted evocative for our delight. Unless my memory is very much at fault, from your café table there is not a single modern building to be seen.

In the immediate foreground is a delightful fountain – the work of Contarini in 1780, when the good times were coming to an end. It is of creamy marble; and, round its rim, little lions couchant, carrying a chain in their mouths, mount solemn guard, for all the world like puppy-dogs retrieving sticks from the water.

One whole side of the square is occupied by the twelfth-century Palazzo della Ragione, with its Gothic windows, its noble outside stair, the roof of which is supported by slender marble pillars, and its massive bell-tower – the Torre del Comune, which is 175 feet (54 m) high. In the beginning this tower was built by the powerful Ghibelline family of Suardi in order to overawe their neighbours – presumably the Guelphs of

Bergamo; and, as its lower courses are about 12 feet (4 m) thick, it must have been quite a convincing argument.

Ghibellines for the Emperor. Guelphs for the Pope. For years fratricidal faction-fights bedevilled every town in Italy. Sooner or later they had to stop. So when the ordinary citizens at last wrested the reins from the rival clans and the Palazzo had become their Broletto or Town Hall, it was decided that, even at the price of submission to a foreign power, law and order must be maintained; and it was then that there appeared above the palace balcony the Winged Lion of the Venetians – that symbol of safety and good government which can still be seen from the coast of Dalmatia almost to the gates of Milan.

At the other end of the Square is the Palazzo Nuovo, which houses a famous library of several thousand volumes. Built in the first years of the seventeenth century, it is arcaded, with a handsome Palladian façade, while inside it is all immense reading-rooms and echoing stone stairs. In such a vast building one can – and I did – become completely lost, creeping from silent room to silent room and being violently 'Ssh'd!' for my pains. Intent on the answer to some query in connection with this book, I pretended not to notice that every head was turned towards me, and aired my faltering Italian to the accompaniment of suppressed giggles from a little group of pretty students. But my carefully prepared sentences did not make the slightest impact and I left the Civic Library as ignorant as when I went in.

If you have not read many books or brochures about Bergamo, prepare for a surprise. As you sat at your café table you will almost certainly have observed beyond the arcade of the Palazzo della Regione, a kaleidoscopic array of many-coloured marbles, so intricate and so elaborate that at a distance, framed in the shadow of the arches, they look more like the contents of some treasure-chest tumbled carelessly on to the ground than the group of exquisite little buildings which is one of the sights of Lombardy. Walk through the arches and you will find yourself in another, smaller square – the Piazza del Duomo; and there before you are Bergamo Cathedral, the basilican church of Santa Maria Maggiore, a baptistry, and what is known as Colleoni's Chapel.

The Cathedral is quite small – a Romanesque building begun in the twelfth century but rebuilt in 1459 and again in the eighteenth century. The façade and cupola are modern. And although the Duomo is richly decorated and contains some interesting pictures, in the opinion of many people it is eclipsed by the neighbouring church of Santa Maria Maggiore.

Santa Maria is an extraordinary building built in 1137 in the form of a Greek cross but much altered in the centuries that followed. It has a huge porch – almost a vestibule – striped horizontally in red and white marble. The canopy above the doorway is supported by pillars of rosy marble resting on the backs of lions, and itself supports two series of life-sized figures of saints and knights in armour – not unlike those miniature champions which slowly and jerkily emerge every hour from certain medieval clocks. There is a famous one at Wells.

The baroque interior is rich and dignified, with a superb golden roof and altar, the former decorated with frescoes. Cool and spacious, it is surprisingly light for an Italian church – which helps one to appreciate six enormous bronze candelabra and some really magnificent wood-carving – notably the screen and choir-stalls, which were the work of Fr. Capodiferro. Kay was particularly impressed by the heavy doors of polished walnut, a series of wonderful marquetry panels, and an elaborate confessional by Andrea Fantoni, one of the greatest wood-carvers that Italy has ever produced. There are also a number of Renaissance paintings and some good Florentine and Flemish tapestries, while in a side chapel you will find the tomb of Gaetano Donizetti.

When reading the stormy history of the Italian city-states, one can hardly fail to be fascinated by the story of the condottieri – those soldiers of fortune with the resounding names: Carmagnola, Gattemelata, Facino Cane, Bande Nere, and our own Sir

John Hawkwood. But to most of us the best known is Bartolomeo Colleoni, whose statue by Verrocchio overlooks the Canal of the Beggars in Venice. Reputed to be the finest equestrian statue in existence, it has gained Colleoni the immortality which he never won with his sword, although he was twice Captain-General of Venice in her war with Milan, and twice commanded the army of Milan against Venice. In those almost bloodless battles of mercenaries, when whole companies could be bought and sold or change sides in the face of the enemy, there was neither hatred nor loyalty, patriotism or over-much courage. War on those terms was simply a matter of selling your sword to the highest bidder – so why cut the throats of men who might soon be your comrades-in-arms? It took the savage Swiss and German *Landsknechte* to transform these knightly passages-of-arms into the bloody, brutal business that they became later.

Colleoni was one of the best – or worst – of these free companions. He played the wicked old game so cleverly and feathered his nest so neatly that when he sheathed his sword his only remaining ambition was to win the applause of posterity. In Venice he had little luck. His pay-masters were too clever for him. He bargained for a statue in front of the Basilica of St Mark – an impossible demand: what he got was a statue in front of the *School* of St Mark, by the church of San Zanipolo and overlooking the Canal of the Beggars.

The fact that he had been tricked did not worry him, for by that time he was dead. But in Bergamo it was a different matter and he achieved his ambition: a castle not far from the city, as his residence, and in the city itself a noble chapel to house his tomb.

The Colleoni Chapel adjoins Santa Maria Maggiore. It was built in the late fifteenth century by Antonio Amadeo and is just the sort of flamboyant edifice which would have been commissioned by a self-made man more used to the camp than to an artist's *bottega*. Yet somehow it comes off. One prepares to sneer but admires instead. The façade may be over-lavish in its chromatic mosaic of marbles – its red-and-white stripes, its medallions, its rose windows and miniature arcades; but one forgets any error of taste when confronted by this overwhelming richness of detail – this profusion of colour and pattern which, when seen from a distance, prompted me to compare it to a heap of precious stones.

The interior is enriched with marquetry, bas-reliefs and paintings, including frescoes depicting the life of St John the Baptist which were executed by Tiepolo nearly 300 years after Colleoni's death. But, thanks to the German woodcarver, Sixtus Siri of Nuremberg, the old warrior is there himself in the shape of a great statue. He is only half-armed but he carries his commander's baton and rides a charger of gilded wood. He must have appeared so hundreds of times at the head of his *condotta.* Of course this statue cannot be compared with Verrocchio's masterpiece in Venice, but it is well done and a fitting adornment for a soldier's tomb.

Bartolomeo Colleoni was a hard man and, in a cruel age, doubtless as ruthless as the eagle that he resembled. But there was another side to his character. That bold, money-grubbing egoist was devoted to his daughter and when his beloved Medea died he had her laid to rest in the chapel that he had prepared for himself. He could do no more for her and in death she repaid the debt by making the whole chapel beautiful. Her effigy is in pure white marble; and, looking at the calm face, it is difficult to imagine a greater contrast to her father's harsh features. She was a slender, delicate-looking girl with one of those graceful, swan-like necks which looked so well in the simple, low-cut gowns of the fifteenth century. Her presence, even in effigy, makes one forget the garish ornament with which she is surrounded and if, as seems probable, she loved her father, there must have been a lot of good in the old freelance after all. He built that fine chapel as a memorial – he who longed to be remembered, but the death of Medea – she was only 16 when she died – broke his heart, and the scholars differ as to whether he was buried there himself.

. . . . .

Near the church you will see a small octagonal building with an angel on top. It is the Baptistry where, in the Middle Ages, total immersion was carried out by those who came to be baptized. It was built in 1340 by another of those gifted men from Lugano – Giovanni da Campione.

Bergamo Alto has been described as a city that is a museum and there are other buildings which, if time permits, the visitor should see: the Citadel, built by the Visconti, the Donizetti Museum, the Risorgimento and Partisan Museum, and the church and cloisters of Sant' Agostino. But even if some of these have to be sacrificed, you should not leave without spending a short time just wandering through the narrow lanes. Between the houses you will catch breath-taking glimpses of the Plain of Lombardy and you will be very conscious of the fact that you are in a medieval walled town. The ramparts are never far away. Some people, even in the old days, must have felt hemmed in: to others, the walls and the watchmen meant safety behind the shield of Venice.

After an argument about parking between our driver and a grim-faced policeman, I had a feeling that the big Neapolitan was not sorry to leave the Upper Town. For quite five minutes he was silent and thoughtful, then his moustache lengthened as he grinned and made some incomprehensible joke about picture galleries.

His meaning soon became clear, however. Just below the Venetian walls, where the New Town begins, he drove us into the grounds of a big eighteenth-century mansion. This was the Accademia Carrara di Belle Arti, founded in 1795 by Count Giacomo Carrara; and it is famous – not for its size, but for the high quality of the paintings exhibited in its 22 rooms. It also carries on an old tradition by providing Bergamo with a school of art at which promising young painters and sculptors are trained.

The Carrara Collection contains among other things choice specimens of the work of Giovanni, Jacopo and Gentile Bellini, of Andrea Mantegna, Boticelli, Raphael and Rubens. There is almost an excess of riches – almost but not quite for, unlike some of the great galleries of Europe, the number of exhibits is not so large that one becomes exhausted and bewildered.

To Kay and me, interested as we are in all things Venetian, the gems of the gallery were two glorious Bellini Madonnas, a portrait of Colleoni, some good Canalettos, and a few of those fascinating 'genre' pictures by Longhi, which bring to life eighteenth-century Venice with its sinister figures in black dominoes and white satin masks. Another small painting which intrigued us was that mysterious 'Portrait of a Gentleman' which some attribute to Giorgione and others to Giovanni Francia, and which many believe to be the only known likeness of the arch-criminal, Cesare Borgia. He was certainly handsome, that Pope's bastard and one can easily imagine the charm which must have masked his insatiable ambition and utter ruthlessness.

The picture that intrigued us more than any other, however, is quite a small one – Bembo's 'Beatrice d'Este and her Court'. Here, in solemn procession, are the very men and women who surrounded Il Moro and his wife in their great red castle of the Sforzas at Milan; and, if they were not so richly dressed, one could picture them in the squares and alleys of the Old Bergamo that we had just left – that is, if it were not for one thing. For this painting holds a little mystery (at least, for us) and, all these months after we saw it, it still nags. There are costumes of black, cream and peacock though, for the most part, the picture is a symphony in red. Yet why – *why* did all the men and women in that procession, including Beatrice herself, have their wrists bound with scarlet cord? Some of the head-dresses are so fantastic that they suggest Byzantium rather than Renaissance Italy. But Constantinople had already fallen to the Turks. So could they be fancy dress? Were those people taking part in one of those masques which were so popular and for which Leonardo da Vinci sometimes designed the settings? Or have those red cords some other significance – possibly religious? No doubt historians know the answer and could settle the question in a few words. But we wondered then what it was all about and we are still wondering. There may be some perfectly simple explanation but, if so, it eludes us.

Verona

Verona – 'La Degna', as the Italians call it – 'the Worthy or Deserving' is a city very much alive. It is a prosperous trade and business centre, yet somehow it contrives to remain a picturesque and lovely place where the past is as vivid as the present. Surrounded by cypress-covered hills, it lies at the foot of the Monti Lessini and is divided by the swift-flowing Adige which sweeps through the city in a great s–bend, reminding one of the Grand Canal in Venice. Indeed, many travellers have discovered the likeness between this city of marble and rose-red brick and her former mistress.

There are several ways of getting to Verona – by air, of course, to the Villafranca Airport, or by train or car over the Brenner Pass. If you are spending a holiday in the Lake District, however, you should remember that the city is within easy reach of the south-eastern shore of Garda – either along State Highway SS 11 from Peschiera or by way of the autostrada which runs from Lazise.

Once, long ago, I stayed in Verona; but the last time I went there, with Kay, we travelled by public transport and I would advise you to do the same. The roads across the plain are neither very beautiful nor particularly interesting, but riding in foreign buses is always worth while. Here in Italy they are fast and efficient; they give you an excellent idea of the countryside and its inhabitants; you are free from *turismo* and all that it implies, and your journey is sure to be enlivened by some amusing 'characters'.

You will never forget your first visit to Verona. Few places in Italy or, for that matter, in Europe can show more monuments of Imperial Rome or the Middle Ages: for beauty and interest second only to Venice is the general verdict. But the importance of Verona today, both from the military and the commercial point of view, still lies as it has always lain, in its situation. Being within easy reach of Lake Garda, in the days of Austrian domination it was the strongest of the four fortress-cities which formed the Lombard-Venetian Quadrilateral. It is the junction of two main arteries of transport by road and rail: that which comes down over the Brenner into Central Italy, and those which cross the Simplon and St Gotthard Passes to serve Milan, Turin, Venice and Trieste.

From the days of its Gallic beginnings, Verona has been a great city. Under Roman rule it flourished exceedingly, as we are reminded by buildings dating from the days of the Caesars; and after the downfall of the Empire, it was the favourite residence of Pipin I, of Odoacer and Theodoric who murdered him. There was a terrible interlude during the tyranny of Ezzolino da Romano – that monster who was puny in body but beside whose atrocities the crimes of the House of Borgia seem mere peccadillos. But all bad things come to an end, and late in the thirteenth century the powerful clan of Scaligeri gained the upper hand and, in spite of a tendency to homicide characteristic of their time, ruled the city wisely and well until they in turn were overthrown by the Visconti of Milan.

There followed a period of internecine strife and bloody feud between the great families until, in 1405, the citizens were wise enough to ask for the protection of Venice. It was the usual story. Incorporated in the Serene Republic, Verona lived in peace until the French invasion at the end of the eighteenth century. After the French, the Austrians; after the Austrians, the red-shirts and freedom from oppression and then, in 1866, an honoured place in the Kingdom of United Italy. Two world wars with an interlude of Fascist rule bring the story up to date, with the emergence of Italy as one of the world's great republics.

When you arrive in the city, at first you will have eyes for nothing but the vast Arena, With the exception of the Colosseum at Rome, it is the largest amphitheatre in the world, dominating Verona as the Cathedral dominates Milan. The huge oval, ringed by 72 arches, is built of solid marble throughout and is capable of seating 25,000 spectators. And the acoustics are perfect. I have been told that when grand opera is performed there, every note can be clearly heard from the topmost tiers of seats.

Built in the first century A.D., the arena was partly destroyed by an earthquake in 1183 but was almost immediately restored. And it has seen every kind of entertainment – if you can call some of them entertainments – from the gladiatorial combats of Ancient Rome and the tournaments of the Middle Ages to the plays and opera of the present day. In 1278, 200 Patarine heretics were burned alive in this place; on the other hand, it has served as a stage for the witty buffoons of the Commedia dell' Arte, and it is the setting for the magnificently produced spectacles which every year attract visitors in their thousands to Verona.

But, for all that, to us it will always be a haunted place. In one of his essays Mr J. B. Priestley suggests that much of the horror of the Roman gladiatorial exhibitions may have been lost on the spectators because the arena was so big: the combatants would have appeared as manikins 'no bigger than my thumbnail'. This may well have been so in the upper tiers; but when Kay and I were in Verona, we were tired after tramping the streets on a very hot day and we sat down to rest in 'ringside' seats almost at ground level. From where we were sitting everything would have been horribly visible – and audible. We would have seen the blood soaking into the sand, and perhaps the struggles of the *secutor* when he realized that he was enmeshed in the weighted net of the *retiarius*; we would have heard only too clearly the roar of the crowd and the swordsman's scream as the deadly trident struck home. I can well believe that grand opera in the Arena is production at its best; but I am afraid that if I was in the audience I would hear through the loveliest aria the baying of a bestial mob and see through the glitter of *Aïda* the eidolon of some unfortunate wretch who died in agony.

Coming out of the amphitheatre, you will find yourself in the Piazza Vittorio Emanuele II, commonly called the Piazza Brà, from the Latin word *pratum,* meaning a field. It is a fine spacious square, planted with trees, and just the right setting for an impressive equestrian statue of that King of Sardinia who became the first King of United Italy. Verona does not forget the Risorgimento. Here, too, are splendid palaces, including the Palazzo Municipale and the Palazzo della Gran Guardia which, when I first visited the city, was being used as the Stock Exchange and Wheat Market. But that was a long time ago.

From here you can follow the Via Mazzini, the main street of Verona and now, happily, a pedestrian precinct. It is lined with shops and offices, and leads to the Piazza delle Erbe – the site of the ancient forum. This is the real heart of Verona and one of the most picturesque and colourful squares in Europe – though, strictly speaking, to call it a square is incorrect: the Piazza is an oblong.

If I am not very much mistaken, your first impression will be of lively bustle and of the laughter and chatter of stall-holders selling everything under the sun. At the same time, it may well be that the mass of gay umbrellas over the stalls may make you think, as we did, of a large field of coloured mushrooms. This colour is carried on by the piles of fruit and vegetables, and even by the surrounding houses. These are of all sorts and sizes, but most of them have balconies which, being the property of Italians, are usually ablaze with flowers. It is no wonder that artists have always loved the Piazza delle Erbe.

There are several interesting monuments to provide these painters with their foregrounds or even with the main feature of their compositions. In the north-east corner is the fourteenth-century Torre del Guardello; and at the side of this tower, occupying one whole end of the Piazza is the Palazzo Maffei, built in 1688. And in front of this great baroque mansion is a tall column bearing the Winged Lion of St Mark. This symbol of the prosperous and happy days of Venetian rule was destroyed by Bonaparte's Frenchmen after the 'Pasque Veronesi' of 1797, when the citizens rose 'en masse' against the invaders and slaughtered them in a manner reminiscent of that other Easter Monday, 500 years before, which became known as the Sicilian Vespers. The Lion of Venice was not replaced until 1886.

In the middle of the market is the Capitello – four ancient columns surmounted by a cupola, while between this monument and the Winged Lion there is a Roman statue of a woman – headless when dug up but now fitted with a marble head and a high spiked crown. For miles around she is reverenced as Our Lady of Verona.

You should see the Palazzo del Comune (1193) – much altered, and the thirteenth-century mansion of the Scaligeri family, during whose overlordship the tragedy of Romeo and Juliet is supposed to have taken place. But, above all, you must not miss one of the sights of the city, another resting-place of the Scaligeri – the tombs. On the east side of the Piazza delle Erbe there are several narrow alleys, one of which is known locally as the Arches. Like us, many Italians are inclined to be reticent about the uglier episodes in their history; but here in the market-place, years ago, one of them told me that Maurice Hewlett was right (in *Little Novels of Italy*) and that this alley once bore a more sinister name – the Volto Barbaro or Horrid Entry, for it was here that Cangrande II, Lord of Verona, was done to death by bravoes hired by his own brother.

As you walk down the lane you will see on your left a delightful little square called the Piazza del Consiglio. Here is a statue of Dante who, at the beginning of his exile from Florence, honoured Verona by becoming the guest of the Scaligeri. The statue, a fine one, is beautifully placed with its back towards what is called the Loggia dei Signori. This is a graceful colonnade of eight arches, with a ledge on which stand the statues of prominent citizens of Verona in the days of the Romans. The upper part of the building is coloured ochre and there are four big windows facing the square. They light the Council Chamber where, when Venice ruled, the local Council of Four used to meet.

Then if you carry on a few yards and under an arch on your right, you will come to the tombs. You will see, built against the north wall of the church of Sant' Antica, the simple tomb of the founder of the Scala dynasty – Mastino I. But I doubt if you will spare it more than a glance, for your attention will be riveted on a splendid collection of statuary. It could almost be called a pageant in stone, for these sepulchres carry you straight back to the Days of Chivalry. Here in their warlike panoply are the great lords of the Scaligeri, mounting guard as they did in life over their city of Verona.

Above the side door of the church you will see a double monument to the best of them all – Cangrande I, renowned for his utter fearlessness and for his ready laughter. He was the friend of Dante, who dedicated *Il Paradiso* to him and he seems to have been comparatively free from the criminal traits which stain the record of his family. Although he was small of stature, they called him the Great Dog and his sepulchre rests on the shoulders of two mastiffs. In the lower monument you see him as he lay in his tomb, his sheathed sword between his clasped hands – the picture of saintly resignation. But above there is a realistic statue of him as he rode to war, with his huge sword – almost as long as himself – bared for action, and his heavy helm with its crest of a hound slung on his back between his shoulder-blades. He is smiling broadly (unusual in a statue) and is a sturdy little figure in his mail, sitting bolt upright on a lugubrious horse which appears to be insane. Both these and other mounted or recumbent effigies were the work of Bonino da Campione, a famous member of that group of artists from the shore of Lake Lugano.

The other tombs are in a marble enclosure. Giovanni della Scala is at the back; but there is a splendid equestrian statue of Cansignorio, the fratricide, who must have had his tongue in his cheek when he ordered his tomb to be executed during his own lifetime and decorated with statuettes of all the Virtues! Opposite to him and near the entrance is Mastino II, Cangrande's nephew – a man mentally unbalanced to the point of homicide, but whose daughter, Beatrice, married Bernabò Visconti and gave her maiden name to La Scala Opera House at Milan. A queer, dangerous breed, but gallant figures in their steel harness. The marble enclosure which surrounds them is reinforced by a fourteenth-century wrought-iron grille which, in its way, is as beautiful and interesting as the statues. It is light and flexible, like mail, and is linked together by the recurring device of the five-runged ladder (Scala), the badge of the clan. It has been suggested that a remote ancestor may have bought or sold ladders, but I find that difficult to believe. In the fifteenth-century it might well have been true: Francesco Sforza, who died Duke of Milan, came of peasant stock; but in those knightly days of the thirteenth, he would have been a brave man who told Cangrande that he was descended from 'base mechanics'. I have sometimes wondered whether some ancestor performed a feat of arms involving a *scaling*-ladder – possibly set against the walls of Acre or Jerusalem. It is just a guess. It have not a shred of evidence. But it suits the temper of the times.

Whether your interest lies in things Roman or in those of the Middle Ages, Verona should satisfy you. It has been said that the Roman remains are the finest in Northern Italy. To begin with, of course, there is that enormous arena which, by itself, is enough to make any city famous. But Verona also possesses a beautiful archway, the Arco dei Gavi – demolished by the French in 1805 and later rebuilt. Then there is the Porta Borsari, which lies on the road leading westward out of the Piazza delle Erbe. Take the turning by the Torre del Guardello and you can hardly miss it. The name comes from the Latin *busarii* or tax-collectors, for once this old gate marked the city boundary and this is where you paid toll. Like so much of Old Verona, it is built of solid marble and consists of a double archway with colonnades and a double row of window openings.

After that, I suggest that you make your way north-east to the Ponte Pietra (the last two arches of the bridge are Roman) and cross it to St Peter's Hill – dominated by the huge fortress of the same name, which was once an Austrian stronghold, and from which there is a fine view of the city and the sinuous curve of the Adige. And on the lower slopes of the hill you will find the Roman Theatre, which is said to be even older than the Arena. For centuries it lay forgotten under the earth while the tide of History flowed over it, and excavation did not begin until 1834. Since then, however, with the help of the Government and the City Corporation, work on the site has been progressing slowly but steadily, bringing to light tiers of seats, corridors and stairs, and many interesting objects of bronze and marble. The best of these smaller finds are on display in the Archaeological Museum which adjoins the Theatre.

And as if all this were not enough, Verona is even richer in relics of the Middle Ages and the Renaissance. Some of these I have mentioned already, but there are enough left to occupy you very pleasantly for some considerable time. To begin with, there are the city walls with their flanking towers – though these ramparts were improved and strengthened as late as the sixteenth century by the great military engineer and architect, Michele Sammicheli, whose statue stands at one end of the Corso Vittorio Emanuele and whose work, it is said, inspired the even more famous Vauban.

You will hardly fail to observe the double arches of the Portoni della Brà (1389) with those fish-tail battlements which are so typical of medieval Italy. You will find them on the south side of the piazza of the same name, between the Palazzo della Gran Guardia and the Museo Lapidario with its wonderful collection of gems. The arches adjoin a pentagonal tower – all that is left of a citadel of the Visconti.

From here you can follow the Via Teatro Filarmonico north-west to where the Adige takes a great sweep to the north by the Arsenal, for it was here, on the west side of the city that the Scaligeri built their stronghold. Their fortress of rose-red brick

– Castelvecchio – is a splendid specimen of an Italian castle, and its towers and ramparts are well worth exploring, especially as the building now houses a museum and picture gallery. Under the Venetians there was a college here, which the Austrians turned into a barracks. Strolling on the walls, one can look down through an embrasure on to one of the most picturesque bridges in Europe – the Ponte Castelvecchio, with its three arches, its battlements and towers. The fortifications were added by Cangrande II and one can imagine his men-at-arms on their tired horses filing over the bridge after some foray. You can imagine it, but I am sorry to say that you would be wrong. During the retreat of the German Army towards the Brenner Pass during the Second World War, the old bridge was blown up. When peace came, however, the Italians restored it and the work was most beautifully done. I have seen both bridges, the old and the new, and I defy anyone but an expert to detect any change.

Some of the richest treasures in Verona's legacy from the Middle Ages are, of course, her many Romanesque and Gothic churches. Quite apart from their religious significance, they are well worth exploring, but as usually – especially on holiday – one's time is limited, it might be as well to concentrate on two of them: the Cathedral and San Zeno Maggiore.

The twelfth-century Cathedral, built on the site of an even older church dedicated to Our Lady, is situated at the extreme northern end of the city, where the river forms a great loop between the Ponte Garibaldi and the Ponte Pietra, so you may think it a good idea to visit it on your way to or from the Roman Theatre.

In 1400 the whole of the upper part of the church, which had been Romanesque, was rebuilt in the Lombard-Gothic style; and, as you can see to this day, the alteration is very obvious. But the Cathedral is a handsome building. The apse is made of 'tufa' – a rough volcanic rock, but the façade is ornamented with a number of small spires which might have detracted from its dignity but which, somehow, are most effective. There is some sculpture, mostly of personages and scenes from the Bible, but the columns of the main doorway are supported on the backs of gryphons or griffins – one of which was the subject of a well-known water-colour by Ruskin. They are most unprepossessing beasts (or should it be birds?) with the heads and wings of eagles and the hindquarters of lions. And above them, on the left and right of the portal respectively, are statues of Roland and Oliver – those paladins of Charlemagne who, according to tradition, took time off from slaying Saracens to endow the original church. To light the façade there is a rose window and two tall side windows, all of which date from the sixteenth century.

The interior, too, is very beautiful. There are three naves, separated by fluted pillars, and the roof of the chancel is covered with frescoes by Francasco Torbido, depicting scenes from the life of the Virgin. The church possesses a wealth of monumental sculptures and paintings – the latter mostly by artists of the Venetian School. They include an Assumption by Titian.

But of all the churches in Verona, the loveliest and most interesting is the basilica of San Zeno Maggiore. At the north-western end of the city, between the river and the ramparts of Theodoric the Ostrogoth, it stands in a great square and is flanked by a lofty rust-red tower with the usual fish-tail battlements. This is the Torre di Pipino, associated with King Pepin, and it once formed part of a palace used as an occasional residence by bishops and other important personages of Church and State.

The San Zeno that we know was built in the twelfth century but, like the Cathedral and so many other churches, it arose on an earlier foundation. Its high campanile is of terracotta inlaid with worked stone and marble, while the façade is comparatively simple – everything leading the eye upwards to a huge rose window. It is one of the earliest known and represents the wheel of fortune.

The lower part of the frontage is covered with bas-reliefs, some of them very old, and these are surmounted by rows of small Romanesque arches which give what otherwise have been a gaunt façade a very elegant appearance. In the lunette or arch above the west doorway is a painted carving of San Zeno the Fisherman, patron saint of Verona; the side architraves are ornamented by symbols representing the months; and on the doors themselves are bronze reliefs of Biblical subjects.

In tune with the façade, the interior of this wonderful church is majestically plain and simple – almost severe. But it is a deceptive simplicity. Having admired the austere beauty of materials and proportions, a closer examination will reveal many objects of interest, many details which provide just the right amount of ornament. The nave and east and west aisles – or, as the Italians seem to prefer to call them, the three naves – are irregularly divided by arches and pillars with varied capitals and are covered by a vaulted wooden roof. The fresco above the central nave is said to be by Giotto, and on the choir-screen are thirteenth-century statues of Christ and the Apostles. The choir is rich with inlaid work and the triptych by Andrea Mantegna above the High Altar has been described as 'one of the noblest paintings of the Renaissance'.

I am sure that you will not want to leave San Zeno without seeing two of its most interesting possessions. The first is another painted statue of the saint and – as is always the case when he is depicted as a bishop – he has a metal fish dangling from a line at the end of his crozier. A curious tribute to one who, like the Disciples, had become 'a fisher of men'.

The second curiosity is near the door, though for many years it was outside the church – and somehow survived. It is the famous porphyry vase which is said to have been bequeathed to San Zeno by the Roman Emperor Gallienus. Just think what that means! It may have been used for washing the feet of pilgrims; but, whatever its purpose, it is a marvel. It has never been in a museum show-case: for 1,700 years it has known the rough-and-tumble of life in a turbulent Italian city. Yet there it is still, almost as good as new – a fragile link with Imperial Rome in the days of her decadence.

And now a word with the sacristan will gain you access to the crypt – if you like crypts. I believe I saw this particular one during my first visit to Verona; but Kay and I much prefer cloisters, which seem to us one of the most charming and civilized forms of architecture, whether they are to be found in a monastery or at one of our older universities. You can plan a brave new world or plot revolution on a campus: the cloisters, more deeply rooted in Time, foster sanity and peace.

Nowadays, I cannot write for long about cloisters without my thoughts going back to that golden afternoon on Lake Como. The cloisters at Piona Abbey are smaller and more luxuriant with trees and shrubs; and I think, to be fair, that they must yield to San Zeno on the score of beauty. They lack the double columns of red marble which support the arches at Verona and there is no view of church or campanile. Neither have they that small but charming square structure of pillars and pantiles which occupies part of the lawn – that green cloister-garth which at home in Chichester has for centuries been called Paradise.

You should linger in the cloisters at San Zeno – and, indeed, in any other cloisters which you may come across in the course of your wanderings. After a few hours spent sight-seeing in the hot Italian sunshine, you will find them as cool and refreshing as the drink which I hope you will enjoy as soon as you have done your duty as a good traveller – or as much of it as can be accomplished in one session of thirst and aching feet. Even a heathen will hardly deny that monks of all times and in all places have learned a lot about tranquillity. But if you doubt me, just say *Buon giorno!* to the first brother you meet. His calm voice and steady eyes will give you your answer – the answer of a man who has found peace in troubled times.

And now, before I take my leave of you, may I suggest that you cross the river to the eastern outskirts of the city, where lies the

Palazzo Guisti and its glorious gardens. It is the gardens that I want you to see, although I have never had the good fortune to do so myself. They were laid out in the sixteenth century and are an example, I am told, of the Italian garden at its best – a pleasance for supple gallants and ladies in farthingales, as stately as peacocks. I think 'elegant' is the word. The gardens are backed by a high hill – a vantage point from which there are vast views across the Plain of Lombardy; there are formal flower-beds, fountains and statues, box hedges, and majestic cypress trees, many of them as old as the garden itself. What better place could there be in which to sit and dream? And, if you are not a thorough-going, dyed-in-the-wool materialist, your dreams in this city of all cities will surely be of young Romeo and his Juliet, and –

Two households both alike in dignity,
In fair Verona where we lay our scene.

So far, I have only made a passing reference to the star-crossed lovers and some of you may have wondered why. My reason is that to do so when talking about Verona usually provokes a snigger from some clever-clever whose self-imposed mission in life is to be a pourer of cold water and whose one ambition is to find an adult who believes in Father Christmas.

The world is in love with tragic lovers and in all its moods from grave to gay – from Hero and Leander to Villikins and his Dinah. But, above all, homage is paid to these young people who lived and loved and died when Verona rang with the clash of steel and the streets echoed with the shouts of the rival factions: 'Capulet! . . . Montague!'

But did Romeo and Juliet ever exist? The denials of the Cold Water Brigade are almost shrill, and certainly the odds are against it. Yet it seems to me not impossible that some old tradition – twisted and warped during its passage through the years – may have given Shakespeare the germ of his tragedy. There are so many earlier versions (not all of them set in Verona) ranging from the stories of Luigi da Porto and

Bandello's *novello*, which was translated into English in 1572, to the present day. We do not know when Shakespeare's play was first performed; but in 1609, 37 years after Bandello's work burst upon London, it is said to have been 'sundrie times publiquely acted by the King's Majestie's Servants at the Globe'.

The point is, was this tragedy founded on fact? I can see no reason why it should not have been. In this city of feuds and civil disorders, when Guelph strove against Ghibelline, when the retainers of Bevilacqua and Ridolfi were at daggers drawn, and when Montecchi and Cappelletti clashed on the slightest pretext – or none, why should not some disastrous love-affair have run its course, ended in the violent death of several of the protagonists, and lingered in the memory of a warm-hearted people.

Those who maintain that Shakespeare's play was founded on a real-life drama say that it took place in the days when Bartolomeo della Scala was Tyrant of Verona – a period rather earlier than that usually shown on the stage; and, true or false, the Veronesi can hardly be blamed for cashing-in on the goldmine that our English Will opened up for them. In the Via Cappello, which is in the very heart of the city, near the Piazza delle Erbe, they will show you the house of the Capulets, complete with balcony. It is built of that delicate rose-red brick which one associates with Verona: it has a good medieval doorway, and ogival windows in the style that has come to be known as Venetian Gothic.

As for the famous balcony – that is of creamy marble, ornamented with a double row of small arches, and there is a convenient plant climbing up the wall – a leafy ladder for a young lover. It can hardly have been there in the Middle Ages and I can hear all the scoffers jeering and saying, 'But was the balcony?' I do not know, though I would say that the odds are heavily against it. I am no architect and for once I am delighted to admit that I cannot judge with any certainty whether this or that specimen of the builder's craft is real or fake. But I am prepared to give my wife the last word. Kay fell completely in love with the house of the Capulets and said very wisely, 'Well, if that isn't Juliet's balcony, all I can say is that it should be!'

The final stage of the Shakespearean's pilgrimage is from Juliet's house to what we are told is her tomb. You will find it down by the river, just south of the Campo di Fiera and not far from the Piazza Brà. There, in the beautiful garden of an abandoned monastery, steps from the cloisters lead down to a vault in which there is a fourteenth-century sarcophagus. Is this really the tomb of Juliet? Is this where it all ended – among the trees and flowers and the softly-cooing doves. It would be pleasant to think so and there are thousands who do – among them those legions of troubled lovers who write to her in the shades and for whom a special 'pillar-box' is provided by the Verona Municipality. It is strange to think that, after all these centuries, Juliet still has a secretary to handle her fan-mail. But so it is, and the number of letters shows no sign of diminishing.

The Guisti Gardens are a good place in which to say goodbye – or, preferably, *Arrivederci!* – to Verona; and Kay and I wish that we could have done so there, instead of at a very ordinary bus stop outside the Arena. As I have said, the views alone would have made it worth while, for from the Gardens you can see both the Alps and the Apennines, though distance veils the Lakes which I hope that you have learned to love.

There they lie, away to the north-west, behind their encircling rampart of hills; and no doubt, in this moment of truth, you will see a sort of composite vision of all that they have meant to you: the maschio tower of Malcesine looming above Lake Garda – the café orchestras of Lugano still churning out 'Torna a Sorrento' as they did years and years before the war introduced it to the Eighth Army – Isola Bella – the Isle of the Fishermen – the friendly monks of Piona – little *luciè* with their awnings spread, riding at anchor in green water – the white wakes of water-ski – sparkling wavelets winking in the sunshine as they come and go – drinks under the vines on hotel terraces – a thousand delectable girls, as dark as night and (dare I whisper it?) better groomed than their sisters in England – while spread at your feet is a panorama of the City of Verona, with all its roofs and towers and bridges, and its broad winding river. Beyond, mile upon mile, stretches the vast Plain of Lombardy.

And somewhere beyond the plain is the rim of the sea and all the islands of Venice.

Index